Number SENSE

Simple Effective Number Sense Experiences

Grades 4–6

Alistair McIntosh

Barbara Reys

Robert Reys

Jack Hope

DALE SEYMOUR PUBLICATIONS®

Managing Editor: Cathy Anderson

Project Editor: Joan Gideon

Production and Manufacturing: Leanne Collins

Illustrative Art: Rachel Gage

Design Manager: Jeff Kelly

Cover design: Lynda Banks

Text design: Nancy Benedict

Published by Dale Seymour Publications®, an imprint of Addison Wesley Longman, Inc.

Order Number DS21802

ISBN 1-57232-263-2

DALE
SEYMOUR
PUBLICATIONS®

4 5 6 7 8 9 10-ML-00 99

This book is printed
on recycled paper.

CONTENTS

INTRODUCTION

Number sense refers to a person's understanding of number concepts, operations, and applications of numbers and operations. It includes the ability and inclination to use this understanding in flexible ways to make mathematical judgments and to develop useful strategies for handling numbers and operations. Number sense results in an expectation that numbers are useful and that mathematics has a certain regularity. A person with good number sense has the ability to use numbers and quantitative methods to communicate, process, and interpret information.

The four-book *Number SENSE: Simple Effective Number Sense Experiences* series is designed to promote thinking and reflection about numbers. The activities help students in primary through middle grades develop number sense through exploring patterns, developing mental-computation skills, understanding different but equivalent representations, establishing benchmarks, recognizing reasonableness, and acquiring estimation skills. Visualization is integral to many activities, as number sense is often developed from visual experiences.

The six sections of this book explore the major components of number sense:

- **Exploring Mental Computation**
  Calculating exact answers mentally, and exploring the thinking that facilitates mental computation

- **Exploring Estimation**
  Working with approximate values to calculate and estimate

- **Exploring Relative Size**
  Developing a sense of the size of a number in relation to other numbers, including benchmarks

- **Exploring Multiple Representation**
  Identifying and using equivalent forms of numbers and expressions

- **Exploring Number Relationships**
  Exploring number patterns and connections between numbers, and understanding the effect of an operation—addition, subtraction, multiplication, division—on two or more numbers

- **Exploring Reasonableness**
  Becoming alert to the reasonableness of a number, solution, or representation, including checks for reasonableness

Each activity falls under one appropriate heading, though most are connected to more than one component of number sense. These interconnections are natural and a reminder that number sense is not a series of disjoint entities but an integration of multidimensional components.

Using the Activities

Each activity is built on the premise that any student can benefit at any time from experiences that encourage them to think about numbers in a sense-making way. The activities can be used in any order, whenever they would be appropriate to anchor, build, and extend students' thinking about numbers in meaningful ways. Most will take from 5 to 15 minutes.

The activities are designed to serve as a source for questions or problems to stimulate thinking and discussion. If the activity is to be presented to the whole class, the activity master may be made into a transparency. Activity masters may also be used to make student copies. When an experience contains more than one activity, begin with the first activity and use the others over a period of time.

Teacher notes explain the intent of each group of activities and suggest ways to present them. The teacher notes contain these components:

- **Number Sense Focus**
  Highlights the main number sense components

- **Number Focus**
  Identifies the types of numbers used in the activity

- **Mathematical Background**
  Describes the rationale or context for the activity, including its connection to different dimensions of number sense—such as relationships of fractions, multiple representation, computational alternatives, and basic facts

- **Using the Activity**
  Offers ideas for preparing students for the activity as well as ways to initiate the experience, questions to raise, and possible directions to take

- **Solutions**
  Provides answers when appropriate and additional insight for some answers

- **Extending the Activity**
  Suggests teacher-directed extensions or variations as well as extensions for students to explore on their own

The Importance of Number Sense

• •

Current reforms in mathematics education emphasize number sense as it typifies the theme of learning mathematics as a sense-making activity. Like common sense, *number sense* is an elusive term that has stimulated discussion among mathematics educators, including classroom teachers, curriculum writers, and researchers. Discussions include lists of essential components of number sense (McIntosh, Reys, and Reys, 1992; Resnick, 1989; Sowder and Schappelle, 1989; Sowder, 1992; Willis, 1990), descriptions of students displaying number sense (or lack thereof) (Howden, 1989; Reys, 1991, 1994), and an in-depth theoretical analysis of number sense from a psychological perspective (Greeno, 1991). Number sense is highly personal. It is related to *what* ideas about number have been established as well as to *how* those ideas were established.

The NCTM *Curriculum and Evaluation Standards* sets forth that children with good number sense have well-understood number meanings, understand multiple interpretations and representations of numbers, recognize the relative and absolute magnitude of numbers, appreciate the effect of operations on numbers, and have developed a system of personal benchmarks.

Number sense exhibits itself in various ways as the learner engages in mathematical thinking. It is an important underlying theme as the learner chooses, develops, and uses computational methods, including written computation, mental computation, calculators, and estimation. The creation and application of algorithms calls upon facets of number sense such as decomposition, recomposition, and understanding number properties. When paper-and-pencil algorithms and calculator algorithms are used, number sense is important as answers are evaluated for reasonableness.

The acquisition of number sense is gradual, commencing long before formal schooling begins. Number sense is often evident at an early age as children try to make sense of numbers. However, growing older does not necessarily ensure either the development or use of even the most primitive notions of number sense. Indeed, although many young children exhibit creative and sometimes efficient strategies for operating with numbers, attention to formal algorithms may actually deter use of informal methods. As students' technical knowledge of mathematics expands, their range of strategies may narrow.

Learned algorithms become the methods most cherished by many students, as they can be executed without much thought. The reaction of a student when asked whether a calculation seems reasonable is often to recalculate—generally using the same method as before—rather than to reflect on the result in light of the context. The lack of a natural inclination to reconsider a calculation is all too common both in and out of school. When selling three items priced at $2.19 each, a clerk reported a total due of $4.88. When the customer responded that the amount seemed too low, the clerk showed no inclination to reflect on the reasonableness of the result. When pressed, the clerk recalculated the amount due. Only when a different total appeared on the register did the clerk recognize an error. While the method of checking (recalculating) is not being questioned, the lack of reflective reasoning is worrisome.

There is evidence that the context in which mathematical problems are encountered influences a student's thinking. For example, while a student may be comfortable in school with a sum of 514 produced by applying a learned algorithm to the computation of $26 + 38$, the same student in a store will likely demand a reexamination if asked to pay $5.14 for two items priced at 26¢ and 38¢.

Students who are highly skilled at paper-and-pencil computations—often the gauge by which mathematics success is measured—may or may not be developing good number sense. When a student reports that $40 - 36 = 16$ or that $\frac{2}{5} + \frac{3}{7} = \frac{5}{12}$, he or she is attempting to apply a learned algorithm but is not reflecting on the reasonableness of the answer. In fact, much of the recent attention to developing number sense is a reaction to overemphasis on computational, algorithmic procedures.

The degree of number sense needed in the world today is greater than ever. Both students and adults encounter a greater range of numbers (government budgets in the trillions of dollars, athletic events timed to the thousandths of a second), in more varied contexts (including graphs and surveys), and encounter more tools (such as computers and calculators) than a generation ago. It might be said that the possession of number sense is the one major attribute that distinguishes human beings from computers. There is every reason to believe that the twenty-first century will demand an even higher level of number sense.

The Teacher's Role in Developing Number Sense

The breadth and depth of students' number sense will grow as they encounter situations that encourage them to reflect on reasonableness, to think about numbers and operations, and to make flexible use of numbers and operations in a variety of situations. Focusing on number sense encourages students to use common sense and to become involved in making sense of numerical situations. *Sense making* is what number sense is all about.

As a teacher, you play a key role in developing your students' number sense by encouraging them to make sense of situations. As activities are explored, spend plenty of time discussing answers and strategies by focusing on questions such as these:

- How did you get your answer?

- Can you explain it another way?

- Did anyone think about it differently?

When there are wrong answers, find out why. Was it faulty reasoning, a computational error, or something else? Sharing how people—including you—thought about the question or problem provides different dimensions of insight into the solution process.

The activities in this book encourage dialogue among students and teachers. We believe that the success of these activities in promoting sense making will be directly related to the quality of the sharing and exchanging of ideas that occurs in your classroom.

References

Greeno, J. G. "Number Sense as Situated Knowing in a Conceptual Domain." *Journal for Research in Mathematics Education* 22 (1991): 170–218.

Howden, H. "Teaching Number Sense." *The Arithmetic Teacher* 36 (1989): 6–11.

McIntosh, A., B. Reys, and R. Reys. "A Proposed Framework for Examining Basic Number Sense." *For the Learning of Mathematics* 12 (1992): 2–8.

National Council of Teachers of Mathematics. *Curriculum and Evaluation Standards for School Mathematics.* Reston, Va.: National Council of Teachers of Mathematics, 1989.

Resnick, L. B. "Defining, Assessing and Teaching Number Sense." In *Establishing Foundations for Research on Number Sense and Related Topics: Report of a Conference,* eds. J. Sowder and B. Schappelle. San Diego, Calif.: San Diego State University, Center for Research in Mathematics and Science Education, 1989.

Reys, B. J., ed. *Developing Number Sense in the Middle Grades.* Reston, Va.: National Council of Teachers of Mathematics, 1991.

Reys, B. J. "Promoting Number Sense in Middle Grades." *Mathematics Teaching in the Middle Grades* 1, no. 2 (1994): 114–20.

Sowder, J. T. "Estimation and Number Sense." In *Handbook of Research on Mathematics Teaching and Learning,* ed. D. A. Grouws, 371–89. New York: Macmillan, 1992.

Sowder J. T. and B. P. Schappelle, eds. *Establishing Foundations for Research on Number Sense and Related Topics: Report of a Conference.* San Diego, Calif.: San Diego State University, Center for Research in Mathematics and Science Education, 1989.

Willis, S., ed. *Being Numerate: What Counts?* Hawthorne, Victoria: Australian Council for Educational Research, 1990.

Exploring Mental Computation

Being able to calculate mentally, without the use of external memory aids (including paper and pencil), is a valuable skill. The illustrations demonstrate that doing computations mentally is often easier, quicker, and more appropriate than performing a written algorithm. One of the benefits of mental computation is that it can lead to a better understanding of place value, mathematical operations, and basic number properties. The cassette tape example $(3 \times \$3.99 = 3 \times \$4.00 - 3 \times 1\cent)$ demonstrates mental application of the distributive property and involves both operations and basic number properties.

Research shows that students tend to rely on written computational algorithms and do not consider mental computation a viable option—perhaps because they have learned that in school, everything must be written. Students need encouragement to develop mental-computation skills and to apply them whenever they are appropriate.

Mental computation lends itself to a variety of thinking strategies. For example, consider these three approaches to calculating how far you can travel on 11 gallons of gas if you get 25 miles to the gallon:

- 25×10 is 250, and 25 more is 275

- 25×4 is 100, so 25×12 is 300, and subtracting 25 is 275

- 25×8 is 200, and 25×3 is 75 more, so the total is 275

As students learn to manipulate numbers in their heads, they develop better number sense and an increased confidence in their mathematical abilities. This confidence will encourage them to consider mental computation as an option when straightforward calculations are encountered. Regular opportunities to develop and apply mental computation not only contribute to number sense, but can significantly improve students' ability to think about numbers in a variety of ways.

Will You Do It in Your Head?

Number Sense Focus

- Number relationships
- Mental computation

Number Focus

- Activities 1–2: Whole numbers
- Activity 3: Fractions
- Activities 4–5: Decimals

Mathematical Background

Research shows that middle-grades students often apply written algorithms to computations that would be more efficient to do mentally. This reliance on pencil and paper probably reflects the emphasis given to written computation in school. Calculators are a powerful computational tool, but wise use of calculators should be encouraged. We should not automatically use a calculator any more than we should automatically use written algorithms.

Using the Activities

These activities give students the opportunity to think about doing computations mentally and to reflect on appropriate computational alternatives. They focus on different operations (addition, subtraction, multiplication, and division) as well as different numbers (whole numbers, fractions, and decimals).

1. In each activity, reveal the top of the transparency. Ask students for other ways to do the computation, and talk about the strategies they suggest.

2. Survey students about which methods they prefer. Encourage them to explain their choice of computation; the sharing of their explanations is the heart of these activities.

3. Next, show the list of problems. Ask students to list the four easiest computations for them to do mentally, and then survey the class for their preferences. Make a list of the "easy" problems offered. Students rarely agree on what is easy, which makes for great discussions—and reminds everyone that people often see the same problem quite differently. Encourage students to explain why they find a particular computation easy.

4. Ask students to list the hardest computation for them to do mentally. Survey and discuss their choices. Students sometimes think a computation is easy when it isn't. For example, in Activity 3, some students may compute $\frac{3}{7} + \frac{2}{3}$ as $\frac{5}{10}$ and report that it is easy! Answers like this offer natural opportunities for follow-up.

5. Focus attention on the idea that the numbers and operations determine the mental computational difficulty. In Activity 1, $370 + 99$ lends itself to mental computation. On the other hand, it is difficult to compute $370 \div 99$ mentally, but easy to estimate if we think about $370 \div 100$. In Activity 2, $450 \div 45$ is an easy mental computation; 450×45 is very difficult.

Extending the Activities

• Ask students to make up a new computation that is easy to do mentally and then explain why it is easy.

• Ask for another computation that is hard to do mentally, and ask students to explain why it is hard.

Will You Do It in Your Head?

Which of these computations are easy for you to do in your head? Why?

1. 430 + 50

2. 750 + 250

3. 370 + 99

4. 100 – 36

5. 357 – 279

6. 548 + 376

7. 800 + 900

8. 1000 – 499

9. 6000 + 6000

10. 864 – 500

11. 855 – 56

12. 456 + 789

Will You Do It in Your Head?

Which of these computations are easy for you to do in your head? Why?

1. 15×4

2. 34×10

3. 7×40

4. 450×45

5. $560 \div 8$

6. $450 \div 45$

7. 60×60

8. 25×48

9. 15×30

10. $24 \times 5 \times 2$

11. 59×1000

12. $16{,}000{,}000 \div 2{,}000{,}000$

Will You Do It in Your Head?

Which of these computations are easy for you to do in your head? Why?

1. $\frac{1}{2} + \frac{1}{4}$

2. $\frac{2}{5} + \frac{2}{5}$

3. $\frac{1}{5} + \frac{1}{6}$

4. $\frac{2}{3} + \frac{2}{3}$

5. $\frac{3}{4} + \frac{3}{4}$

6. $\frac{1}{2} + \frac{5}{6}$

7. $1 - \frac{1}{3}$

8. $1\frac{1}{2} - \frac{3}{4}$

9. $\frac{1}{2} - \frac{1}{3}$

10. $2 - \frac{3}{4}$

11. $\frac{3}{7} + \frac{2}{3}$

12. $1\frac{1}{2} + 2\frac{3}{4}$

Will You Do It in Your Head?

Which of these computations are easy for you to do in your head? Why?

1. 0.5 + 0.25

2. 0.75 + 0.75

3. 0.234 + 0.789

4. 1.14 + 0.5

5. 1 – 0.45

6. 0.5 – 0.25

7. 0.407 – 0.188

8. 1.001 – 0.45

9. 0.632 – 0.5

10. $0.75 + $0.75

11. $1.14 + $0.50

12. $1.00 – $0.45

Number SENSE / Grades 4–6

Will You Do It in Your Head?

Which of these computations are easy for you to do in your head? Why?

1. 0.2×30

2. 24×0.5

3. 8×0.25

4. 0.25×0.8

5. 0.33×0.22

6. 0.8×0.7

7. 0.800×0.700

8. 0.45×0.55

9. 0.68×0.59

10. 70×0.50

11. $70 \times \$0.50$

12. $8 \times \$0.25$

EXPERIENCE 2

Today's Target

Number Sense Focus

- Mental computation
- Number relationships

Number Focus

- Activities 1–2: Whole numbers, fractions, decimals

Mathematical Background

When we calculate mentally, we frequently use relationships between numbers to simplify the calculation. To add 24 + 47, for example, we could use the relationship 47 = 50 − 3 and calculate 24 + 50 − 3. The ability to quickly see the relationship between one number and many other numbers helps us to choose calculation strategies.

Using the Activities

In these activities, students are presented with a target number and are invited to create calculations, meeting certain requirements, for which the target number is the answer.

1. Show the top part of the transparency so the target number is visible. Ask for some calculations that would produce the target number.

2. Reveal each restriction in turn, and ask for calculations of this type that would produce the target number.

3. Use Activity 2 in the same way, except you or your students choose a target number (whole number, fraction, or decimal).

Extending the Activities

• •

- Invite students to challenge the class with a restriction of their own for the given target number.

- Create other restrictions and other target numbers, such as the date or the day of the year.

- Challenge the class to work individually to write as many calculations as possible in a given amount of time (say, 2 minutes) that produce the target number. To encourage creativity, make a rule that a calculation will score only if no one else in class has thought of it.

Today's Target

Today's target is **12**

Try to make today's target in each of these ways.

1. Adding two numbers

2. Finding the difference of two numbers

3. Multiplying two numbers

4. Dividing one number by another

5. Adding three numbers

6. Multiplying three numbers

7. Multiplying and subtracting

8. Using a fraction

9. Using a decimal

10. Doing it an unusual way

Today's Target

Today's target is ☐

Try to make today's target in each of these ways.

1. Adding two numbers

2. Finding the difference of two numbers

3. Multiplying two numbers

4. Dividing one number by another

5. Adding three numbers

6. Multiplying three numbers

7. Multiplying and subtracting

8. Using a fraction

9. Using a decimal

10. Doing it an unusual way

EXPERIENCE 3

Compatible Numbers

Number Sense Focus

- Mental computation
- Number relationships

Number Focus

- Activities 1–3: Whole numbers

Mathematical Background

Numbers that are easy to compute mentally and seem to go together naturally are called *compatible numbers*. For example, 16 + 84 and $\frac{1}{4} + \frac{3}{4}$ are compatible numbers for addition; 25 × 8 and $\frac{1}{3} \times 24$ are compatible numbers for multiplication. Sets of numbers totaling a multiple of 10 are useful compatible numbers for addition. To solve 84 and 28, we may reason that 84 + 16 = 100, and 12 more makes 112. We can also use compatible numbers to find the sum of several numbers. For example, to add 4 + 3 + 8 + 7 + 6, we may reason that 4 + 6 = 10, and 3 + 7 = 10, and 20 + 8 = 28. Compatible numbers help simplify mental computations.

Using the Activities

In these activities, students are shown a 6-by-6 grid of whole numbers and are challenged to identify sets of two or more adjacent cells—horizontally or vertically—with a given sum.

1. Show the transparency, and explain that the challenge is to find two or more adjacent numbers either vertically or horizontally (not diagonally) that add to the given sum.

2. Invite students to identify sets of numbers, and circle them as they are identified. Remind students that they can use each number in only one combination.

Solutions

Activity 1	Activity 2	Activity 3

Activity 1

4	7	9	8	12	3
7	9	17	3	7	9
6	11	4	6	13	8
7	5	8	3	4	7
6	13	8	11	4	5
14	2	10	10	12	8

Activity 2

13	6	31	24	9	41
30	15	35	26	39	11
20	28	3	19	36	8
4	22	47	31	14	16
7	25	12	33	17	26
39	25	38	16	25	9

Activity 3

17	46	15	39	8	62
83	24	57	43	46	38
5	29	66	22	46	25
23	87	45	43	72	5
28	13	55	35	28	55
49	6	94	19	81	15

Extending the Activities

• •

- For one or more of these activities, you may wish to make copies for students to mark individually instead of using a transparency or after you have used the transparency with the class. There is more than one way to make sums on each grid.

- Have students create their own grids for compatible numbers and exchange them with others to solve.

Compatible Numbers

Find two or more numbers in a row, across or down, with a sum of 20.

4	7	9	8	12	3
7	9	17	3	7	9
6	11	4	6	13	8
7	5	8	3	4	7
6	13	8	11	4	5
14	2	10	10	12	8

Compatible Numbers

Find two or more numbers in a row, across or down, with a sum of 50.

13	6	31	24	9	41
30	15	35	26	39	11
20	28	3	19	36	8
4	22	47	31	14	16
7	25	12	33	17	26
39	25	38	16	25	9

Compatible Numbers

Find two or more numbers in a row, across or down, with a sum of 100.

17	46	15	39	8	62
83	24	57	43	46	38
5	29	66	22	46	25
23	87	45	43	72	5
28	13	55	35	28	55
49	6	94	19	81	15

How Many Cubes?

Number Sense Focus

- Mental computation

Number Focus

- Activities 1–3: Whole numbers

Mathematical Background

The abilities to visualize and to count in a spatial setting are valuable number sense skills. For example, suppose a 3-by-3-by-3 cube is shown with cubes missing from each visible corner, and it is assumed that they are also missing from the corners not visible. To devise a strategy for counting all the cubes, we must analyze the visible parts of the structure, mentally construct those parts not visible, and mentally subdivide the structure into countable parts.

Using the Activities

In these activities, students are shown drawings of structures made with cubes and are asked to calculate the number of cubes in each structure. In some drawings, not all cubes are visible; students must visualize them by continuing the pattern established by the visible cubes.

1. In Activity 1, show the first drawing, and invite students to calculate the number of cubes in the structure. You may need to emphasize that they should not estimate the number of cubes, but find a strategy for mentally calculating the number of cubes. Allow them plenty of time. It may be helpful for students to work in pairs and share strategies.

2. Use the remaining drawings in Activity 1 and the drawings in Activity 2 in the same way.

3. In Activity 3, make sure students understand that not all the cubes in the structure are visible, but that they should assume the cube pattern they can see also holds for the areas not visible.

4. Ask individuals or pairs to share their answers and to explain their strategies. Students have shared these strategies for Activity 3:

- "Since there are nine cubes in the front layer, and there are 3 layers, I saw that $3 \times 9 = 27$."

- "It looked like a cube with its corners missing. If it were a cube, it would have $3 \times 3 \times 3$ cubes = 27 cubes, but it looks like 8 corner cubes are missing, so there are only 19 cubes."

- "I can see a cross of 5 cubes in front, and I think there must be another cross behind, which makes 10 cubes. In the middle is a 3-by-3 square, which is 9 more cubes, so that's 19 cubes in all."

Solutions

It is possible that other legitimate answers could be supported. When reasonable explanations are provided, the answer should be accepted.

Activity 1	Activity 2	Activity 3
1. 16	1. 18	1. 27
2. 30	2. 24	2. 20
3. 25	3. 24	3. 19
4. 36	4. 56	4. 19

Extending the Activities

- Have students build their own structures and challenge a partner to count the number of cubes used and to explain their counting strategy.

How Many Cubes?

How many cubes are in each figure?

1.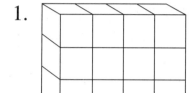

2.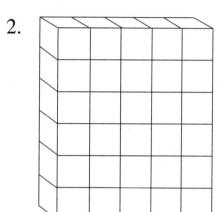

3.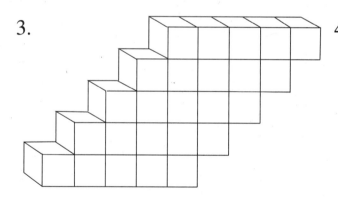

4.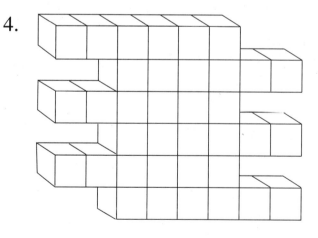

How Many Cubes?

How many cubes are in each figure?

1.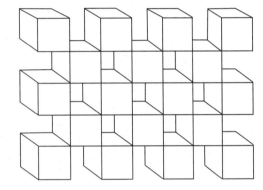

2.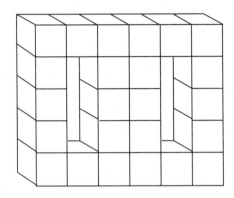

3.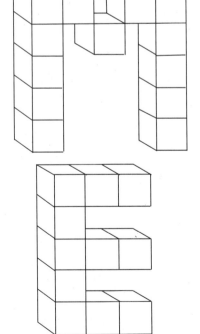

4.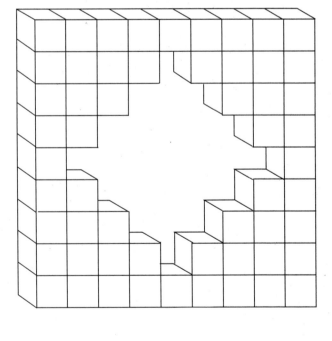

How Many Cubes?

How many cubes are in each figure?

1.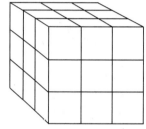

2.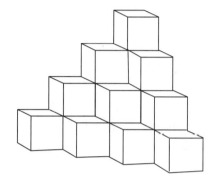

3.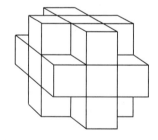

4.

EXPERIENCE 5

•••••••••••••••••••••••••••••

Different Dollars

Number Sense Focus

- Mental computation
- Multiple representation

Number Focus

- Activities 1–3: Whole numbers, decimals

Mathematical Background

•••••••••••••••••••••••••••••••••

Money lends itself naturally to mental computation. Countries around the world have different systems of currency, but several–for example, Australia, Canada, and the United States–use dollars. The dollars look different and have different buying power. Experiences with different dollars provide a multicultural connection and encourage students to think about relationships between currency systems.

Using the Activities

•••••••••••••••••••••••••••••••

1. In Activity 1, ask students the value of each bill and coin shown and to identify the coin worth the most and that worth the least.

2. Offer an example of an equivalent relationship, such as that a dime is equivalent to two nickels, or two quarters make a half dollar. Encourage students to explain how they determined the total amount of money shown. Ask what one bill is worth more than this amount.

3. As a warm-up for Activity 2 or 3, ask whether anyone has traveled to another country and, if so, whether they have any foreign currency to show or tell about.

4. After Activity 2 or 3, ask students to discuss differences and similarities in the monetary systems of Australia, Canada, and the United States. Help them understand that although all three countries use dollars and cents, and all have a 10¢ coin, they have different coins. For example,

Australia has no 1¢ or 25¢ coin, and the Canadian dollar is a coin rather than a bill.

Solutions

Activity 1

1. $5, $2, $1, 50¢, 25¢, 25¢, 10¢, 10¢, 10¢, 5¢, 1¢, 1¢, 1¢
2. most: half dollar; least: penny
3. Possible answer: Two dimes and one nickel are worth a quarter.
4. $9.38

Activity 2

1. $5, $1, 25¢, 25¢, 10¢, 10¢, 10¢, 5¢, 1¢, 1¢, 1¢
2. most: $1 coin (looney); least: penny
3. Possible answer: Two 10¢ and one 5¢ coin are worth one 25¢ piece.
4. $6.88

Activity 3

1. $5, $1, 50¢, 20¢, 10¢, 10¢, 10¢, 5¢
2. most: two dollar; least: 5¢ piece
3. Possible answer: One 20¢ piece is worth two 10¢ pieces.
4. $9.05

Extending the Activities

• •

- As a class, make a list of all the paper bills minted in the United States.

- Point out that Australia has no pennies, and discuss what would happen if pennies were no longer minted in the United States.

- Ask students to find out which is worth more—a Canadian dollar or a United States dollar—based on today's exchange rate. How about a Canadian dollar and an Australian dollar? A United States dollar and an Australian dollar?

- Tell students that a book selling for $14.95 in Austin, Texas, sells for $18.99 in Toronto, Ontario. Using today's exchange rate, which book is the better buy?

Different Dollars

1. Identify the value of each bill and coin shown.

2. Which coin is worth the most? Which is worth the least?

3. What equivalent relationships do you see?

4. What is the total amount of money shown? Explain how you determined your answer.

Different Dollars

1. Identify the value of each bill and coin shown.

2. Which coin is worth the most? Which is worth the least?

3. What equivalent relationships do you see?

4. What is the total amount of money shown? Explain how you determined your answer.

Different Dollars

1. Identify the value of each bill and coin shown.

2. Which coin is worth the most? Which is worth the least?

3. What equivalent relationships do you see?

4. What is the total amount of money shown? Explain how you determined your answer.

Choose Your Strategy

Number Sense Focus

- Mental computation
- Multiple representation

Number Focus

- Activities 1–3: Whole numbers

Mathematical Background
••••••••••••••••••••••••••••

Seeing the big picture to make sense of a task at hand is a part of developing number sense. For example, in evaluating $5 \times 47 \times 2$, it is possible to compute 5×47 mentally and then double the result, but the big picture suggests an easy alternative: $5 \times 2 \times 47$. Although the commutative and associative properties are the foundation for this alternative, what's most important is that it *makes sense*. Students need to learn that mathematics *should* make sense and that when they see an easy way to solve a problem, they should use it.

Using the Activities
••••••••••••••••••••••••••••

The computations in the activities can be done in many ways.

1. Show just the computation to be done, and ask students how they would do it. Encourage them to explain their thinking.

2. If any of the strategies shown on the bottom of the transparency are different from those shared by students, reveal the strategies and ask students to discuss them.

3. To promote further discussion, ask questions such as these:

   - Describe the thinking and computation each student used.

   - Which method do you think is the easiest? Why?

- Which method do you think is the hardest? Why?

- Which method do you prefer for this problem? Why?

Solutions

Students will probably have several explanations for how each computation can be done.

Activity 1

If students are ready for more specific vocabulary to describe the processes used in these strategies, you may want to point out that Tisha first decomposed the numbers and then mentally multiplied the parts.

Activity 2

You may want to discuss how Tomas used the relationship of 4 as 2×2 to double 13 twice, but that his approach got too complex to be done mentally. When this happens, we need to think of alternatives. Rachel chose *compatible factors* to multiply 4×25, then did 13×100. Daniela applied a *doubling strategy* to 25 twice and got an easy factor (100) to multiply by 13.

Activity 3

You may want to review with students that Meela computed 8×20 mentally, then *decomposed* 160 into $100 + 60$ and multiplied each factor times 25–requiring her to keep several numbers in short-term memory. Noah thought of 8 as double 4, and was able to multiply 4 times 25 and then double the result to get 200. He multiplied the *lead digits* and kept track of the zeros necessary for the result.

Extending the Activities

- Ask students how they might compute $2 \times 467 \times 5$ or $34 \times 40 \times 50$ mentally.

- Give students other computations, involving three or more factors, that can be done mentally.

- Ask students to make up a computation, involving three or more factors, that can be done mentally.

- Write $36 \times 45 \times 21 \times 0$ on the board, and ask students to compute the answer mentally. Ask them why is it helpful to look at the entire computation before beginning.

Choose Your Strategy

How many cubes are in this building?

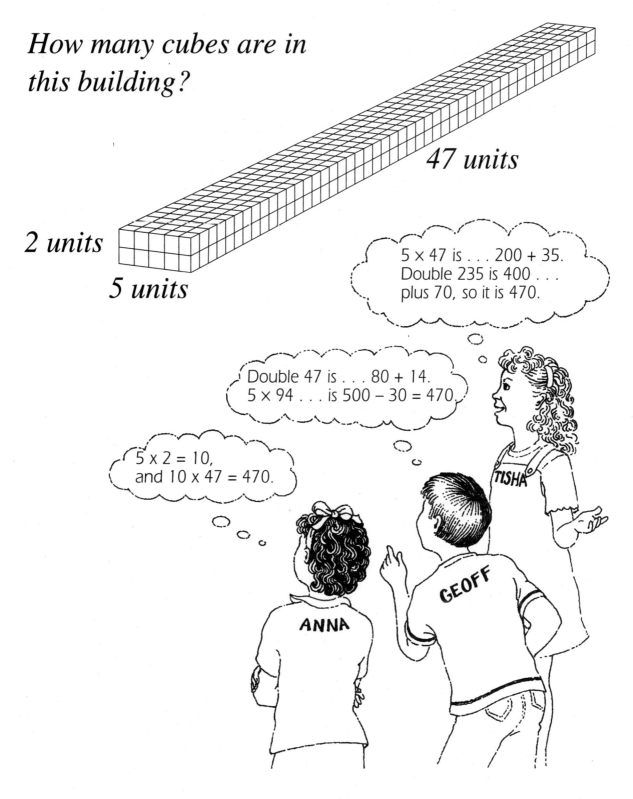

47 units

2 units

5 units

5 × 47 is . . . 200 + 35.
Double 235 is 400 . . .
plus 70, so it is 470.

Double 47 is . . . 80 + 14.
5 × 94 . . . is 500 − 30 = 470.

5 × 2 = 10,
and 10 × 47 = 470.

TISHA

GEOFF

ANNA

Choose Your Strategy

How many cubes are in this building?

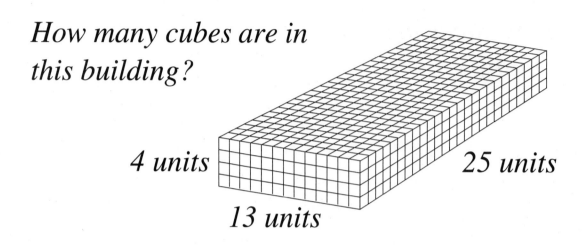

4 units   25 units

13 units

Choose Your Strategy

How many cubes in this building?

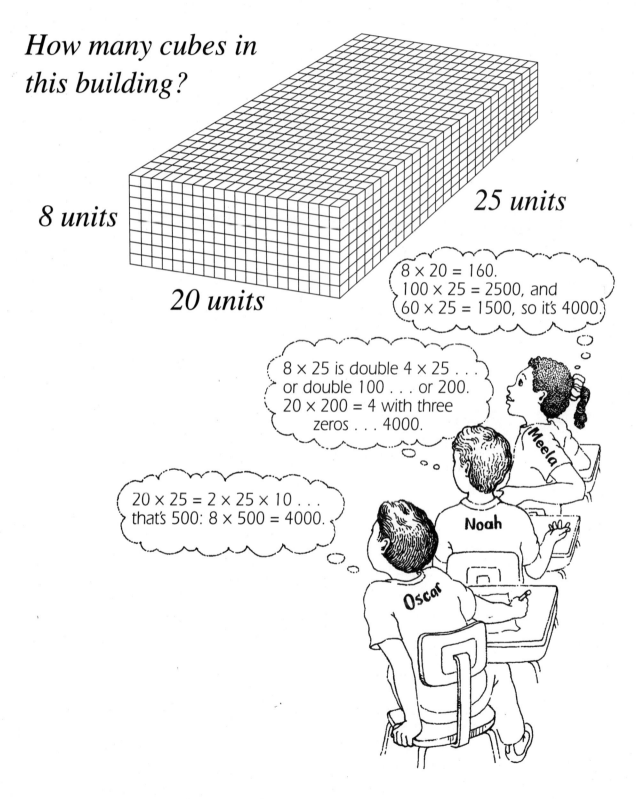

8 units

25 units

20 units

8 × 20 = 160.
100 × 25 = 2500, and
60 × 25 = 1500, so it's 4000.

8 × 25 is double 4 × 25 . . .
or double 100 . . . or 200.
20 × 200 = 4 with three
zeros . . . 4000.

20 × 25 = 2 × 25 × 10 . . .
that's 500: 8 × 500 = 4000.

Meela

Noah

Oscar

EXPERIENCE 7

Multiplying Powers of Ten

Number Sense Focus

- Mental computation
- Number relationships

Number Focus

- Activities 1–2: Whole numbers

Mathematical Background

Multiplying by 10 and powers of 10 are easy mental computations; it is actually inefficient to write such computations down or to use a calculator. Mentally computing with powers of 10 encourages students to think about the numbers and to search for patterns or relationships among them. Students should learn to look for opportunities to use powers of 10 in computations.

Using the Activities

If students are not yet aware of patterns that apply when multiplying by powers of 10, you may want to use calculators to demonstrate multiplying by powers of 10. (The purpose of using calculators here is to facilitate pattern recognition, not to establish reliance on calculators to perform such computations in the future.)

1. In Activity 1, reveal each list of factor pairs, and ask students to compute the products mentally and then describe the relationships and patterns they used to compute each product. For example, a student might reason that 5×10 is the same as five $10 bills, or $50, or that 5×100 can be thought of as five $100 bills, or $500. Encourage students to make connections and to use the patterns they discover.

2. As you reveal the lists of factors at the bottom of the page, encourage the exploration of patterns and relationships. For example, 130×10 and 131×10 produce products that differ by 10; 130×100 and 131×100 produce products that differ by 100. Ask students why these relationships

exist. Check to make sure they treat computations that involve the same digits (such as 405×10 and 450×10) properly, as place-value errors are common.

3. In Activity 2, continue the exploration of patterns with powers of 10. For example, 40×6 is the same as $4 \times 6 \times 10$. Since we know $4 \times 6 = 24$ and we know how to multiply by 10, we know that $4 \times 60 = 240$. Similarly, 30×7 is the same as 3×70, and 30×70 must be 10 times greater than 30×7.

Solutions

Answers to the problems are given here, but the focus of this experience is the relationships and patterns that students discover.

Activity 1

1. 40; 800; 140; 50; 500
2. 400; 8000; 1400; 5000; 180
3. 270; 4500; 510; 5100; 51,000
4. 130; 1300; 1310; 13,000; 13,100
5. 450; 4500; 4050; 40,500; 40,600
6. 170; 1070; 10,700; 17,000; 17,100

Activity 2

1. 60; 240; 6400; 630; 3500
2. 210; 2100; 210; 1800; 18,000
3. 100; 300; 4000; 3000; 10,000
4. 500; 2000; 420; 4200; 4200
5. 320; 3200; 3200; 1600; 160,000
6. 180; 1800; 2000; 12,000; 82,000

Extending the Activities

• •

- Ask students to list five two-digit numbers. Then, ask them to multiply each number by 10 (or 100 or 1000).

- Ask students to decide which equivalent computation in each of the following pairs would be easiest to do mentally:
  $2 \times 17 \times 5$ *or* 10×17 $5 \times 34 \times 2$ *or* 10×34 $25 \times 46 \times 4$ *or* 100×46

- Ask students to write other pairs of equivalent multiplication computations.

Multiplying Powers of Ten

1. 4×10

   100×8

   14×10

   10×5

   5×100

2. 4×100

   8×1000

   100×14

   1000×5

   18×10

3. 10×27

   100×45

   51×10

   51×100

   51×1000

4. 13×10

   10×130

   131×10

   130×100

   100×131

5. 10×45

   450×10

   10×405

   405×100

   406×100

6. 17×10

   10×107

   107×100

   100×170

   171×100

Multiplying Powers of Ten

1. 10×6

    40×6

    8×800

    90×7

    700×5

2. 30×7

    30×70

    3×70

    200×9

    2000×9

3. 2×50

    6×50

    8×500

    500×6

    5000×2

4. 5×100

    5×400

    6×70

    700×6

    70×60

5. 8×40

    400×8

    40×80

    40×40

    400×400

6. 18×10

    100×18

    200×10

    60×200

    82×1000

EXPERIENCE 8

Sorting Products

Number Sense Focus

- Mental computation
- Estimation
- Relative size

Number Focus

- Activities 1–3: Whole numbers

Mathematical Background

The ability to compute products mentally develops with regular opportunities to do mental computation. Once students compute a product, it is important that they think about the relative size of the answer. These activities combine mental computation and the ordering of numbers by their relative size.

Using the Activities

1. As a warm-up, copy this illustration onto the board:

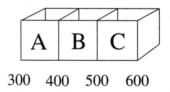

300   400   500   600

Explain that the drawing shows how numbers can be sorted into each box–for example, numbers between 300 and 400 can be put into Box A. Ask students to name several numbers that belong in each box. What is the largest number that can be placed in Box B? The smallest number? These questions address what to do with values falling on a boundary, such as 400. Different answers can be defended; the important issue is to decide on a consistent plan for handling boundary values.

2. Either make a copy of each activity for students, or ask them to draw lines on a piece of paper (such as __ __ __ __ __ __ __ __), where the number of lines is equal to the number of boxes shown. In each activity, ask students to decide which product goes where and to write the correct letter in the boxes. Have them describe how they solved the problems, and encourage a variety of explanations.

Solutions

Activity 1

1. NICE JOB

2. YOU DID IT

Activity 2

1. RIGHT ON

2. ON TARGET

Activity 3

1. IN YOUR HEAD

2. THAT'S ALL

Extending the Activities

• •

- Ask students to propose other computations that belong in a particular box.

- Ask students to make up computation problems that have a result between certain values–such as 500 to 600; 5000 to 6000; or 50,000 to 60,000–and explain how they constructed their problems.

- Have students construct a series of mental computations that will reveal a secret message.

Sorting Products

1. Decide in which box each letter should be placed. Explain your decisions.

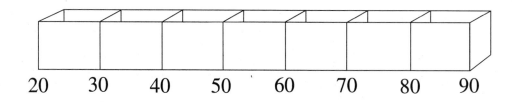

20   30   40   50   60   70   80   90

$N = 7 \times 4$ $O = 9 \times 8$ $I = 8 \times 4$ $J = 7 \times 9$

$C = 7 \times 6$ $E = 7 \times 8$ $B = 9 \times 9$

What is the message?

2. Decide in which box each letter should be placed. Explain your decisions.

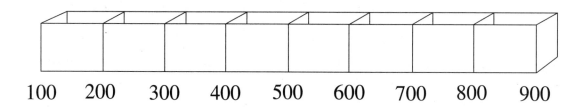

100   200   300   400   500   600   700   800   900

$U = 60 \times 6$ $I = 70 \times 8$ $Y = 20 \times 6$ $D = 8 \times 80$

$I = 90 \times 8$ $O = 30 \times 9$ $D = 80 \times 6$ $T = 90 \times 9$

What is the message?

Sorting Products

1. Decide in which box each letter should be placed. Explain your decisions.

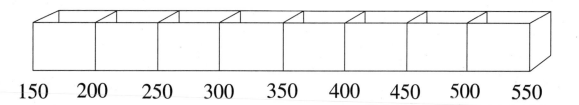

150   200   250   300   350   400   450   500   550

$H = 40 \times 8$ $T = 60 \times 6$ $I = 60 \times 4$ $R = 8 \times 20$

$O = 80 \times 6$ $N = 9 \times 60$ $G = 40 \times 7$

What is the message?

2. Decide in which box each letter should be placed. Explain your decisions.

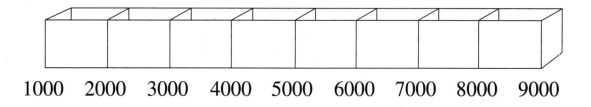

1000   2000   3000   4000   5000   6000   7000   8000   9000

$O = 200 \times 6$ $G = 800 \times 8$ $A = 500 \times 9$ $T = 500 \times 7$

$E = 800 \times 9$ $T = 900 \times 9$ $R = 800 \times 7$ $N = 600 \times 4$

What is the message?

Sorting Products

1. Decide in which box each letter should be placed. Explain your decisions.

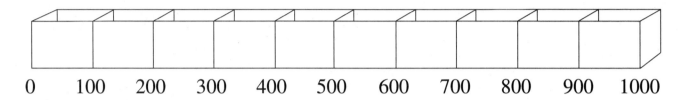

0   100   200   300   400   500   600   700   800   900   1000

$D = 99 \times 10$ $I = 33 \times 3$ $Y = 26 \times 10$ $N = 18 \times 10$ $O = 60 \times 6$

$U = 20 \times 24$ $E = 80 \times 9$ $R = 26 \times 20$ $H = 30 \times 21$ $A = 42 \times 20$

What is the message?

2. Decide in which box each letter should be placed. Explain your decisions.

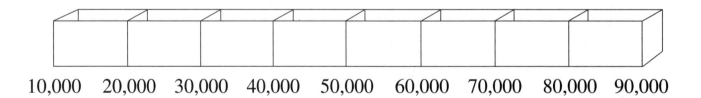

10,000   20,000   30,000   40,000   50,000   60,000   70,000   80,000   90,000

$A = 700 \times 90$ $T = 900 \times 50$ $S = 800 \times 70$ $A = 500 \times 70$

$L = 90 \times 800$ $T = 9000 \times 2$ $L = 900 \times 90$ $H = 600 \times 40$

What is the message?

Postage Stamp Math

Number Sense Focus

- Mental computation
- Number relationships

Number Focus

- Activities 1–3: Whole numbers

Mathematical Background
· ·

The ability to decompose and recompose (that is, break down and build up) numbers in different ways is a valuable skill. Sheets of stamps are natural array models for skip counting and multiplication, and they provide a setting for exploring relationships among multiplication facts.

Using the Activities
· ·

In these activities, students will build on the knowledge they already have to do new problems; for example, they might use their knowledge of 5×5 and 2×5 to solve for 7×5.

1. If any students collect stamps ask them to share what they know. You might get into a discussion of sheets of stamps. Are they a standard size? Are there the same number of stamps in each sheet? (No, both sheet size and number depend on the size of the stamps.)

2. In Activity 1, ask students to describe how to find the value of each group of stamps. The value of the block of 6¢ stamps, for example, might be determined by calculating 2 x 3 x 6¢, whereas the strip of 4¢ stamps is worth 5 x 4¢; note that the model produces the notation. Ask: Which group costs the most. (10¢ and 1¢ are each 40¢.) Which could you use to send a letter? Explore the questions at the bottom of the transparency.

3. Show the Activity 2 transparency for about 10 seconds, then turn off the overhead. Ask students to estimate the amount of money this sheet of

stamps is worth and to explain how they got their answers. Some students may confuse the total *number* of stamps with their total *value*.

4. Show the transparency again, and confirm the number of rows and columns. Reveal a few rows or columns at a time, and ask students to determine the cost of the stamps that are visible and to explain their thinking. Encourage different methods of calculating the values.

5. Show the Activity 3 transparency for several seconds, then ask students to estimate the number of stamps and how they got their answers.

6. Mask stamps to reveal certain arrays. For example, show a 4-by-6 array and ask for the value of the stamps showing. Encourage various calculation methods, such as these:
   - "$4 \times 10¢ = 40¢$ per row, and there are six rows, or $2.40."
   - "$6 \times 10¢ = 60¢$ per column, and there are four columns, or $2.40."
   - "$4 \times 6 = 24$ and $24 \times 10¢ = \$2.40$."

7. Connect any of the above activities to money. For example, when skip counting, you might say "5 dollars," "10 dollars," and so on. Write several representations of what is said aloud; five dollars can also be written as $5 or $5.00

Solutions

Activity 1

1. The four 10¢ stamps and the forty 1¢ stamps both cost 40¢; the four 5¢ stamps and the five 4¢ stamps both cost 20¢.

2. Possible answer: Four 10¢ stamps, forty 1¢ stamps, and four 5¢ stamps.

3. Possible answer: Three 8¢ stamps and four 5¢ stamps.

Extending The Activities
• •

- Have students call or visit a post office to research what stamp values can be bought.

- Ask students whether two given sheets of stamps—for example, an 8 by 4 sheet of 25¢ stamps and a 10 by 10 sheet of 8¢ stamps—cost the same amount.

Postage Stamp Math

1. Which groups cost the same amount of money?

2. If you spent exactly $1, which groups of stamps did you buy?

3. If you spent $0.50 and received a penny and a nickel in change, which stamps did you buy?

Postage Stamp Math

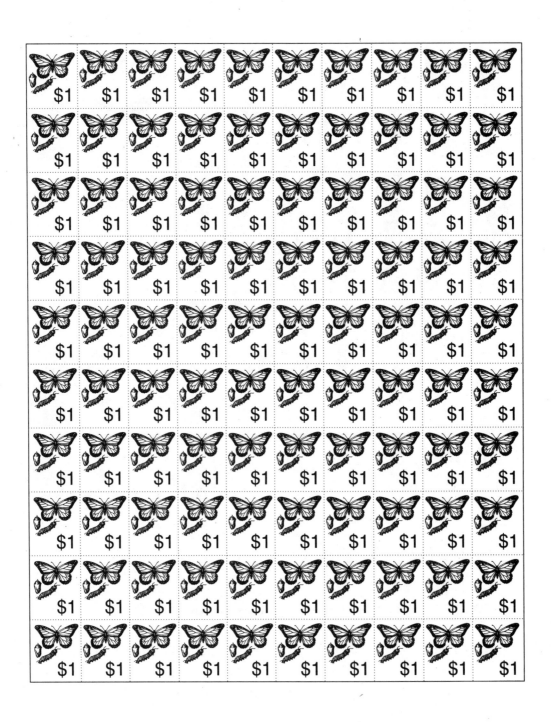

Postage Stamp Math

EXPERIENCE 10

Choose Your Path

Number Sense Focus

• Mental computation

Number Focus

• Activities 1–5: Whole numbers

Mathematical Background

Mental computation helps us to think about numbers, to recognize numbers that are easy to compute, to apply mathematical properties, and to explore relationships. For example:

• $(2 + 5) \times 3$ produces a different result from $(2 \times 3) + 5$.

• A factor of 0 always produces a product of 0.

• $5 \times 5 \times 4$ is easy to compute mentally.

These activities provide opportunities to practice mental computation in an intriguing and challenging context.

Using the Activities

In these activities, it helps to have a paper copy of the mazes to record thinking; you may want to distribute a copy of the mazes to each student.

1. In Activity 1, make sure students understand the rules and that they realize that everyone is to begin at the left with the same Start Number, 40. Ask whether any two paths will produce the same result. Students may suggest that $40 \times 4 + 5$ and $(40 + 5) \times 4$ have the same result. As they check this conjecture, talk with them about the order of operations.

2. Ask students to answer the questions about this maze.

3. Follow a similar procedure for Activities 2 and 3.

4. The blank mazes in Activities 4 and 5 can be used in several ways.

  - Provide a Start Number or Finish Number, and have students fill in the remaining values and operations.

  - Provide both a Start Number and Finish Number, and have students fill in the values and operations. This task is not easy as all paths must produce the Finish Number.

As students share a variety of answers, everyone will be exposed to the idea that there are many possible solutions.

Solutions

Activity 1

1. $(40 + 5) \times 4 = 180$
2. $(40 + 10) \times 3 = 150$
3. $40 \times 4 + 5 = 165$
4. Possible answer: Change the +5 in the middle path to +10, which gives a path of $(40 + 10) \times 4 = 200$.

Activity 2

1. Answers will vary.
2. $0 \times 25 \times 10 + 7 = 7$
3. $(0 + 10) \times 8 \times 4 = 320$
4. $0 \times 50 \times 2 \times 4 = 0$

Activity 3

1. Answers will vary.
2. $(25 \times 4 - 50) \div 5 + 25 = 35$
3. $(25 - 5 + 0) \times 8 + 40 = 200$
4. Possible answers: $25 \times 4 \div 4 \times 2 + 5 + 25 = 80$, $25 \times 1 \times 2 + 5 + 25 = 80$

Extending the Activities

• •

  - Ask students to change the Start Number and observe how the Finish Number changes.

  - Point to a particular maze, and ask students whether they can change one operation at a particular step to produce the greatest result, which operation it would be, and why it would work.

  - Challenge students to create their own mazes.

Choose Your Path

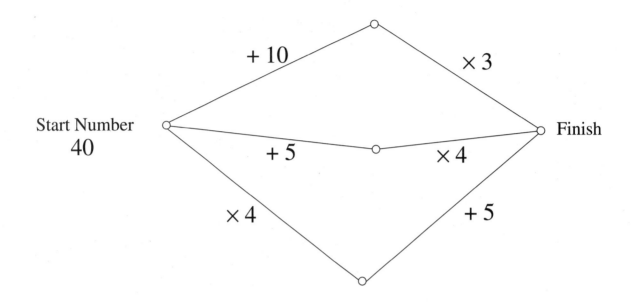

Rules:
a. *Begin at the Start Number.*
b. *Use each result in the next step.*
c. *Work your way to the right.*
d. *Do not retrace or move left.*

1. Which path has the greatest result?

2. Which path has the least result?

3. Which path has a result of 165?

4. Change exactly one number so that a path will have a result of 200.

Choose Your Path

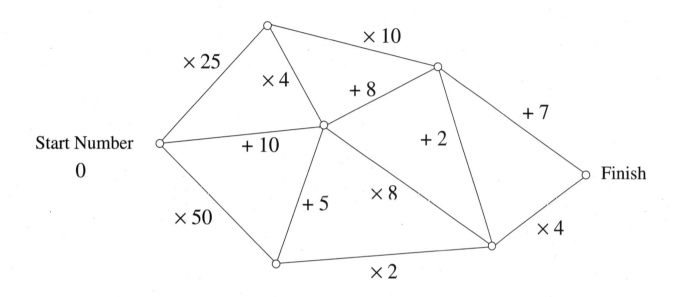

Start Number
0

Finish

Rules:
a. *Begin at the Start Number.*
b. *Use each result in the next step.*
c. *Work your way to the right.*
d. *Do not retrace or move left.*

1. Trace three different paths. Find the result of each path.

2. Find a path with a result of 7.

3. Which path has the greatest result?

4. Which path has the least result?

Choose Your Path

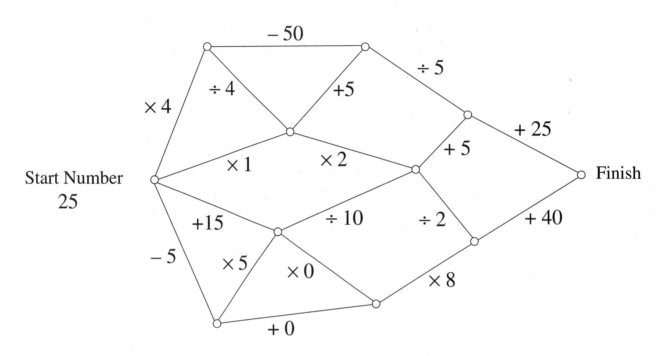

Rules:
a. *Begin at the Start Number.*
b. *Use each result in the next step.*
c. *Work your way to the right.*
d. *Do not retrace or move left.*

1. Trace three different paths. Calculate the result of each path.

2. Find a path that has a result of 35.

3. Which path has the greatest result?

4. Which path has a result of 80?

©Dale Seymour Publications®

Choose Your Path

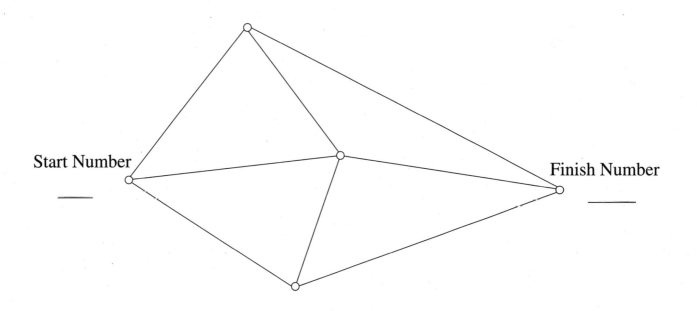

Start Number

_____

Finish Number

_____

Rules:

a. *Begin at the Start Number.*
b. *Use each result in the next step.*
c. *Work your way to the right.*
d. *Do not retrace or move left.*

Choose Your Path

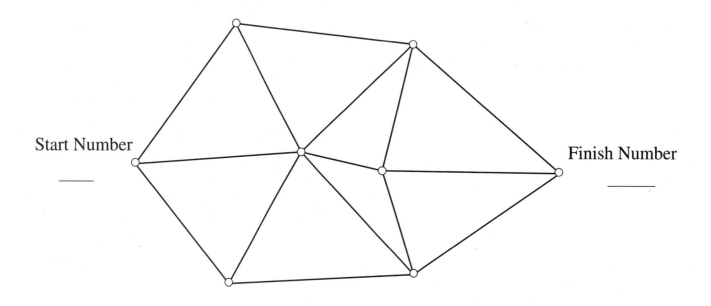

Start Number

_____

Finish Number

_____

Rules:
a. *Begin at the Start Number.*
b. *Use each result in the next step.*
c. *Work your way to the right.*
d. *Do not retrace or move left.*

Number SENSE / Grades 4–6

Exploring Estimation

Estimates are useful when exact answers are impossible, unrealistic, or unnecessary. Measurements such as length, area, capacity, volume, distance, and time are approximations; they can be made more accurate by using a smaller unit, but they are always estimates. Estimation is about producing answers that are close enough to allow for good decisions without making extremely precise measurements or doing elaborate, exact computations.

The first step in developing estimation skill is to learn to recognize whether a particular situation requires an exact answer or an estimate, and the degree of accuracy needed. When timing a slow-cooking casserole, half an hour more or less may not be crucial; when using a microwave, seconds matter. Deciding whether to estimate and how closely to estimate encourages, promotes, and rewards high-level mathematical thinking.

Estimation strategies are quite different from those we employ when an exact answer is needed. One valuable estimation technique is relating the estimate to a referent, or benchmark, that we know—such as the height of one story of a building, or the capacity of a milk carton. People with good number sense use a variety of personal benchmarks.

Research has shown that estimation employs mental computation, rewards flexible thinking, challenges students to think about numbers in ways that are meaningful for them, develops an awareness of multiple strategies, encourages a tolerance for error, and builds an appreciation of the power of inexact values in making decisions. The development of estimation skills helps dispel the one-right-answer syndrome often associated with exact computation. Research has also shown that students are often reluctant to estimate because they are more comfortable with exact answers. Thus they are unaware of how powerful estimation can be, both in and out of school.

The activities in this section will help students develop an appreciation for estimation and will challenge them to think about what numbers to use and how to use them.

How Full Is It?

Number Sense Focus

- Estimation

Number Focus

- Activity 1: Fractions
- Activity 2: Decimals
- Activity 3: Percents

Mathematical Background

Students become familiar with estimating capacity at a very early age. At home, "How much do you want?" and "How much will it hold?" are common questions, and the answers to them are generally estimates.

Using the Activities

In these activities, students estimate what fraction, decimal, or percent of a glass contains liquid. A measuring rule is given as a guide.

1. In Activity 1, reveal only the first glass. Invite students to estimate what fractional part of the glass contains liquid, using the marking on the side as a guide. Encourage them to describe their strategies (for example, "I could tell it was a little less than full, so I thought it must be about $\frac{4}{5}$").

2. Show each of the other glasses in turn, and ask the same question. Show the rule with the other glasses only if students are having difficulty, as the focus of this lesson is estimation. Encourage students to estimate an answer and to think of the rule as they make a connection to an appropriate fraction. For example, if it is a little less than $\frac{1}{2}$ full, then $\frac{2}{5}$ is a good estimate; $\frac{3}{5}$ isn't.

3. In Activity 2, ask students to give their estimates as decimals.

4. In Activity 3, ask them to give their estimates as percents.

Solutions

Use these values as a guide; accept any reasonable estimate.

Activity 1

1. $\dfrac{4}{5}$, $\dfrac{2}{5}$, $\dfrac{5}{5}$, $\dfrac{3}{5}$

2. $\dfrac{2}{7}$, $\dfrac{5}{7}$, $\dfrac{3}{7}$, $\dfrac{6}{7}$

3. $\dfrac{8}{11}$, $\dfrac{5}{11}$, $\dfrac{3}{11}$, $\dfrac{9}{11}$

Activity 2

1. 0.3, 0.5, 0.9, 0.2
2. 0.9, 0.6, 0.4, 0.7
3. 0.75, 0.05, 0.25, 0.45

Activity 3

1. 80%, 50%, 10%, 70%
2. 20%, 60%, 0%, 40%
3. 95%, 55%, 75%, 5%

Extending the Activities

- Have students estimate the part of each glass that is empty.

- Ask students to find pictures of partially filled glasses, vases, or other containers and to estimate the part filled.

- Challenge students to draw glasses filled to a given fraction, decimal, or percent.

How Full Is It?

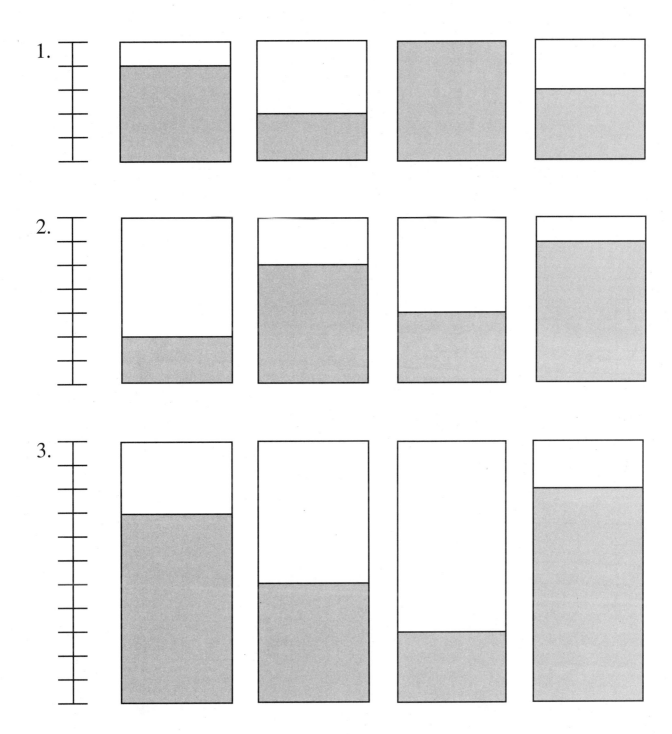

How Full Is It?

1.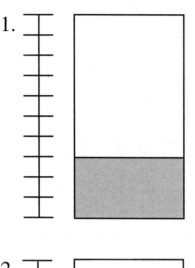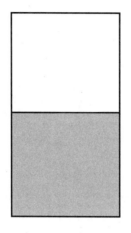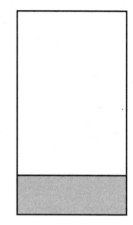

2.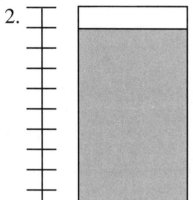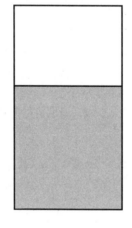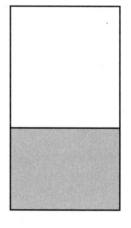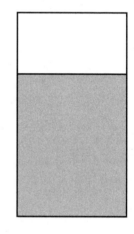

3.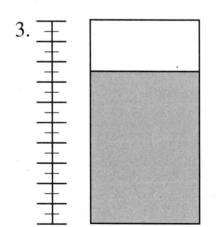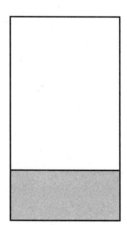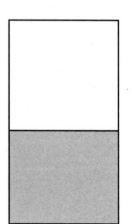

How Full Is It?

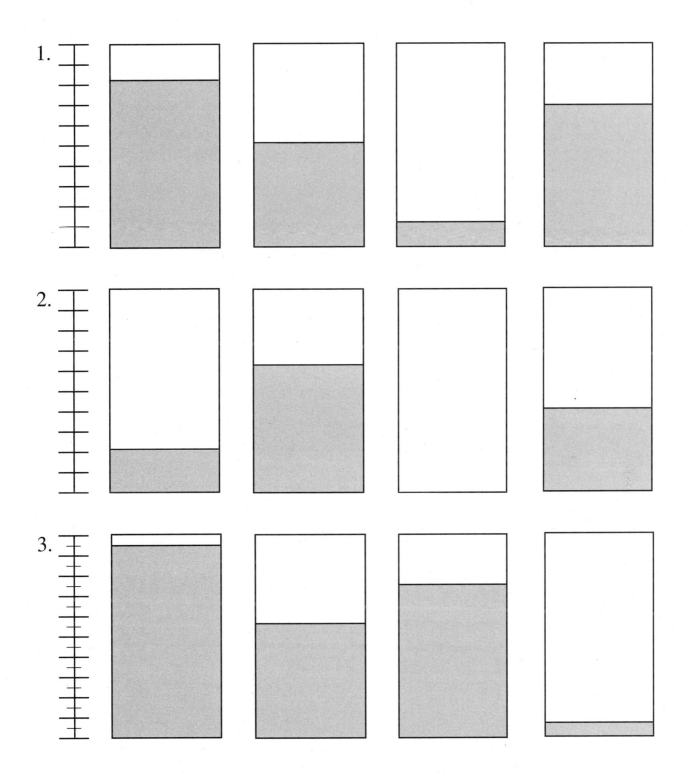

EXPERIENCE 12

What Percent Are. . . ?

Number Sense Focus

- Estimation
- Mental computation

Number Focus

- Activities 1–3: Percents

Mathematical Background

Students need a meaningful understanding of percent. In these activities, they develop a sense of percent by exploring strategies for visually estimating percentages. Students are shown a collection of gray cubes and white cubes and are asked to estimate what percent are white. They are challenged to do this not by counting but by observing the whole collection, estimating the part that is white, and representing their estimate as a percent.

Using the Activities

There are several ways to estimate the quantities in each activity. Accept any reasonable estimates.

1. In Activity 1, explain that you will display a set of 100 cubes, all of which are either white or gray, for about 5 seconds. Show the first set of cubes, then ask students to estimate the percent of the cubes that are white and to explain their estimation strategy; for example:

   - "I think there are less than $\frac{1}{4}$ white, so I estimate less than 25% white."

   - "I think there are at least twice as many gray cubes as white cubes, so less than $\frac{1}{3}$ are white. I think they are about 30% white."

2. You might want to demonstrate other ways to estimate. For example, estimate the percent of white cubes in only part of the collection.

3. In Activity 2, explain that each set contains 20 white cubes, while the number of gray cubes varies.

4. In Activity 3, make sure students recognize that each set contains 100 cubes.

Solutions

How estimates are made is the focus of these activities. Exact values are given to provide you with a quick check for reasonableness.

Activity 1

1. 15% white (15 white out of 100)
2. 35% white (35 white out of 100)
3. 50% white (50 white out of 100)
4. 75% white (75 white out of 100)

Activity 2

1. 40% white (20 white out of 50)
2. 50% white (20 white out of 40)
3. 25% white (20 white out of 80)
4. 80% white (20 white out of 25)

Activity 3

1. 80% white (80 white out of 100)
2. 40% white (40 white out of 100)
3. 56% white (56 white out of 100)
4. 70% white (70 white out of 100)

Extending the Activities

• •

- Show collections of real cubes of two or three colors, and invite estimates of the percent of each color in the collection.

- Give students a 10-by-10 grid of squares, and have them color the squares with two or three colors. Invite the class to estimate the percent of each color in each design.

What Percent Are. . . ?

Estimate what percent of each set of cubes is white. Each set contains 100 cubes.

1.

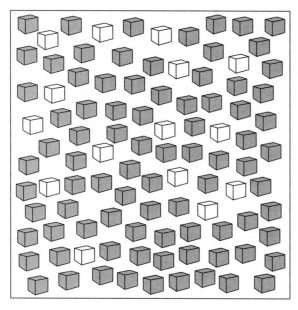

2.

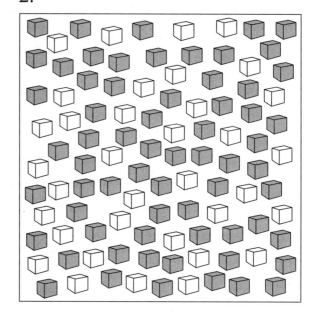

3.

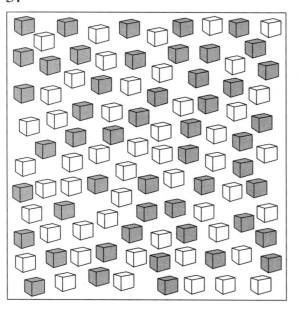

4.

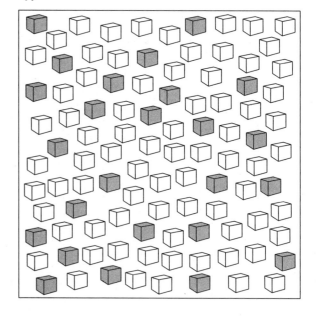

Number SENSE / Grades 4–6

What Percent Are. . . ?

Estimate what percent of each set of cubes is white. Each set contains 20 white cubes.

1.

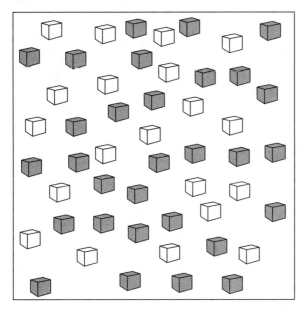

2.

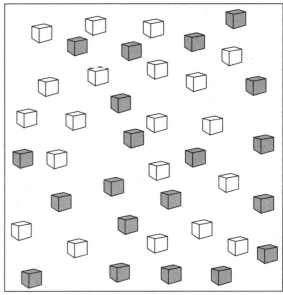

3.

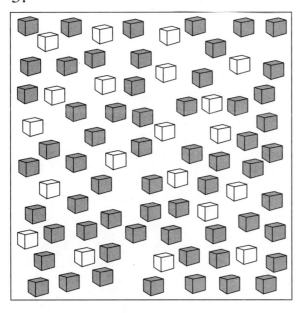

4.

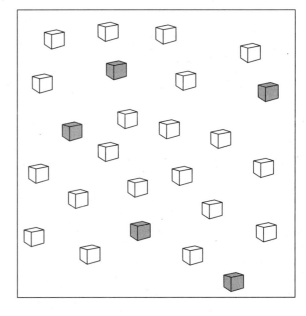

What Percent Are. . . ?

Estimate what percent of each set of cubes is white.

1.

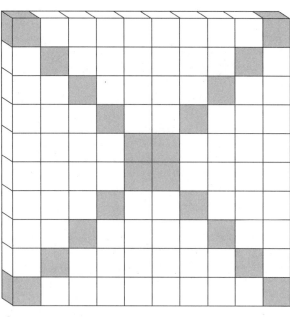

2.

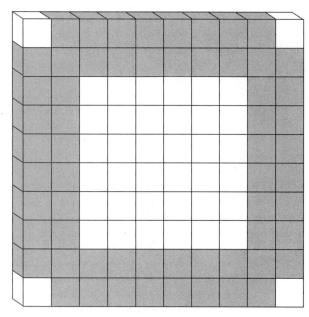

3.

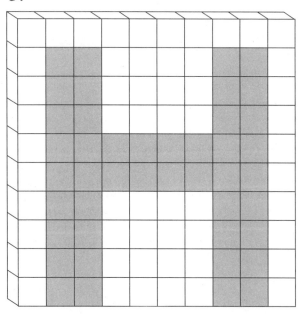

4.

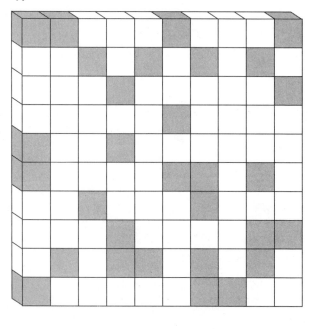

Number SENSE / Grades 4–6

About How Many Do You See?

Number Sense Focus

- Estimation
- Mental computation

Number Focus

- Activities 1–3: Whole numbers

Mathematical Background

Estimating is a complex process that requires thinking about numbers in many different ways. Benchmarks, or perceptual anchors, are powerful estimation tools. A *benchmark* is a quantity whose size is readily perceived in different settings. For example, if you look at a stadium of people and estimate that 500 people are in one section, 500 can serve as a benchmark for estimating the total number of people in the stadium. Although the goal of estimation is to produce reasonable estimates, what is reasonable depends on the situation. Students need to develop a tolerance for error and recognition of when an exact answer may be difficult or impossible to find.

Using the Activities

The value of these activities is the richness of the discussion generated as students share with each other how they estimated the numbers of objects in the illustrations.

1. Show the Activity 1 transparency for about 30 seconds. Ask students to estimate the number of lady bugs they saw. To do this, they need to estimate how many rows and columns of lady bugs there are.

2. Ask students to explain how they arrived at their estimates; for example, students have given these explanations: "I estimate about 15 across and 20 down, so I think there are about 300." "It is less than 20 by 30, so my estimate is less than 600." These responses both indicate powerful mathematical thinking.

3. Make a list of the different estimation methods students share and the estimates each produce.

4. The coins in Activity 2 are not arranged in an array, so the estimation task is somewhat more difficult. Show the transparency for 30 seconds, then ask about how many dimes students see and how they made their estimates.

5. Once students have made estimates of the number of dimes, you might take advantage of the context to encourage mental computation. For example, ask: About how much money is that? About how many nickels is that?

6. In Activity 3, the birds are not uniformly sized or distributed. The estimation task is more challenging but still provides opportunities to apply the principle of benchmarks. For example, an estimate of the birds in part of the picture may be used to make an estimate of all of the birds.

Extending the Activities

- Ask students to estimate the number of ceiling tiles or floor tiles in the room.

- Ask students to estimate the number of bricks along one side of a building.

- Ask students to estimate the number of blades of grass in a square foot of lawn.

About How Many Do You See?

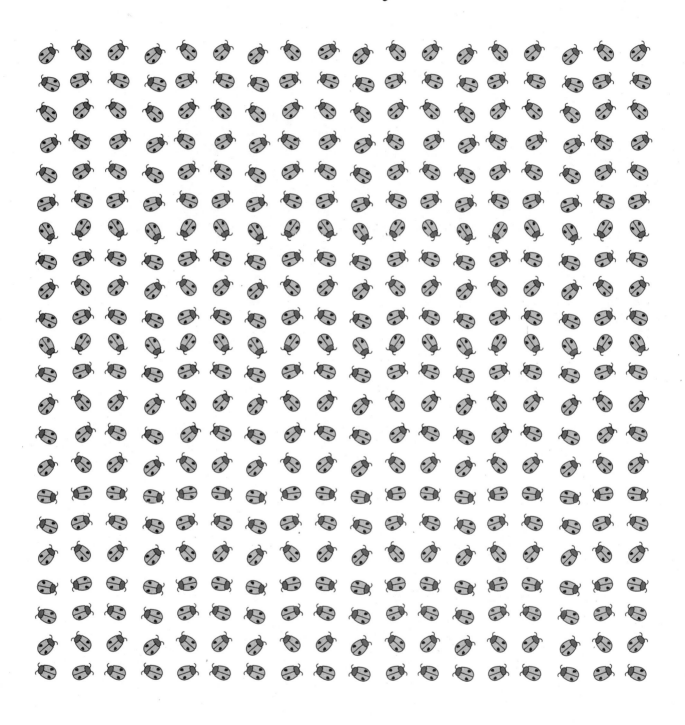

About How Many Do You See?

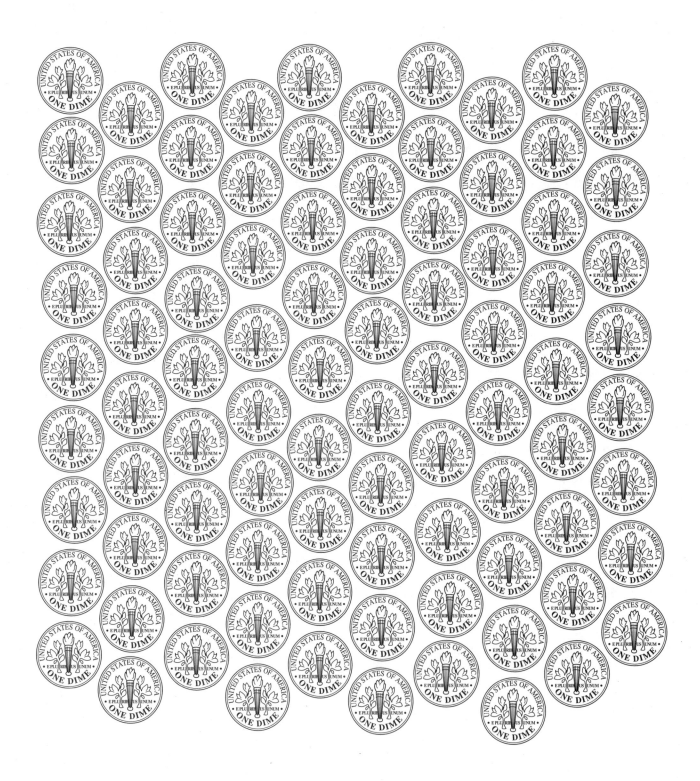

Number *SENSE* / Grades 4–6

About How Many Do You See?

EXPERIENCE 14

About How Many Is It?

Number Sense Focus

- Estimation
- Number relationships

Number Focus

- Activity 1: Whole numbers
- Activities 2, 3: Decimals

Mathematical Background

Many estimates can be made by using numbers that are close to actual values. Using compatible numbers, for example, you might reason that $2485 \div 77$ is more than 24 because $2485 \div 100$ is more than 24. While better estimates exist, dividing by 100 is quick and easy. On the other hand, you might reason that $2485 \div 77$ is about $2400 \div 80$ or $2100 \div 70$. Each method produces a good estimate quickly, and neither uses traditional rules for rounding, which might produce $2500 \div 80$ or $2000 \div 80$; instead, they involve rounding to compatible numbers, or numbers that are convenient to use.

Using the Activities

These activities encourage students to consider the operation and the numbers involved and round to numbers that simplify the computation.

1. As a warm-up, ask students their birth weight. List the weights. Was everyone the same birth weight? Estimate the average birth weight of the students who do know their birth weight. Ask: Is your birth weight related to your current weight? Are you now double your birth weight? Ten times? Twenty times?

2. In Activity 1, be sure students realize that some weights are reported in grams and others in kilograms. (You might check on their knowledge of the relationship between grams and kilograms.) Ask students to answer

the questions—which ask for estimates, not exact calculations—and then to share how they arrived at their answers and how they used compatible numbers in making their estimates.

3. In Activities 2 and 3, again have students answer the questions and explain how they made their estimates. In Activity 3, a range of values is reported because a single value is inadequate—another reminder of the inexactness often encountered in the real world.

Solutions

Any reasonable estimate is acceptable. The process used to produce the estimate and the related discussion are more important than the specific answers.

Activity 1

1. about 2 to 3
2. about 150 to 200
3. about 4
4. about 80 to 150
5. about 90 to 110

Activity 2

1. about 4 to 5 times
2. from 5 to 10 years of age
3. from 1 to 10 years or from 5 to 15 years of age
4. from 10 to 15 years of age
5. about 15 to 20 times

Activity 3

1. about 2.5 to 3 times as long
2. about 3 to 5 times as long
3. about 2 to 3 times as long
4. between 0.3 m and 0.8 m taller
5. about 6 to 8 times as long

Extending the Activities

• Ask students to research the birth weight and adult weight of other creatures, and discuss their growth patterns.

• Present, or have students locate, a weight/height growth chart, and ask students to create estimation problems related to the chart.

About How Many Is It?

Animal Weights

	Elephant	Lion	Leopard
Birth weight	about 90 kg	1200 to 1500 g	500 to 600 g
Adult weight	about 5500 kg	120 to 180 kg	50 to 65 kg

1. The birth weight of a lion is about how many times the birth weight of a leopard?

2. The birth weight of an elephant is about how many times the birth weight of a leopard?

3. At 9 months, an elephant weighs about 340 kg. About how many times its birth weight is a 9-month-old elephant?

4. About how many times its birth weight is an adult lion?

5. About how many times the weight of an adult leopard is the weight of an adult elephant?

Number SENSE / Grades 4–6

About How Many Is It?

Growth of a Typical Girl

Age	infant	1 year	5 years	10 years	15 years
Weight	3.6 kg	10.2 kg	16.9 kg	31.8 kg	56.7 kg

1. About how many times her birth weight is a 5-year-old girl?

2. During what 5-year period does a girl typically double her weight?

3. During what 10-year period does a girl typically triple her weight?

4. During what 5-year period does the greatest weight gain typically occur?

5. About how many times her birth weight is a teenage girl?

About How Many Is It?

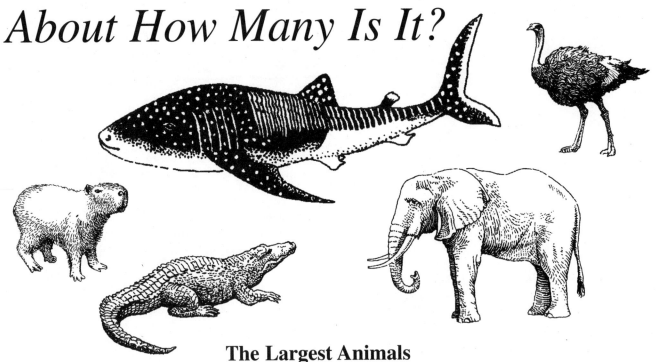

The Largest Animals

Type	Animal	Size
Largest mammal	Blue whale	30 to 34 m long
Largest land animal	African bush elephant	3 to 3.2 m tall
Largest bird	North African ostrich	2.4 to 2.7 m tall
Largest fish	Whale shark	11.5 to 13 m long
Largest reptile	Crocodile	4.3 to 4.9 m long
Largest rodent	Capybara	1 to 1.4 m long

1. A blue whale is about how many times as long as a whale shark?

2. A crocodile is about how many times as long as a capybara?

3. A whale shark is about how many times the length of a crocodile?

4. An African bush elephant is about how much taller than a North African ostrich?

5. A blue whale is about how many times as long as a crocodile?

Picture It!

Number Sense Focus

- Estimation
- Relative size

Number Focus

- Activity 1: Whole numbers
- Activity 2: Fractions

Mathematical Background

We encounter ordered numbers every day. Street numbers help us locate houses and businesses. Graphs usually have benchmarks to help with the interpretation of the displayed information. The more benchmarks are recognized and used, the easier an ordering task becomes.

Using the Activities

In these activities, students decide what information they can obtain from a portion of a number line.

1. In Activity 1, display the number line, and ask students to make a list of some things they know for sure from the picture. If they need help getting started, you might ask: Which is longer, the Amazon or the Nile? How do you know? Which river is longer than 5000 miles?

2. Show the map, and ask where each river is located. You might provide the actual lengths of the rivers to confirm some of the students' conclusions: Nile River, Africa, 4145 miles; Amazon River, South America, 4000 miles; Yangtze River, Asia, 3915 miles long; Mississippi River, North America, 2340 miles.

3. In Activity 2, students locate lengths on a number line and make a list of some things they can see from their picture. If they need help getting started, you might ask: Which is longer, B or D? How do you know? You might provide fraction names—$\frac{2}{10}$, $\frac{4}{10}$, $\frac{6}{10}$, $\frac{8}{10}$, and $\frac{9}{10}$—and ask

them to match the fraction with the bars and explain their decision.

4. Ask how many days it took each strand of hair to grow. (You may use a transparent ruler to demonstrate these fractions—the graph is 10 cm long, so each 1 cm mark corresponds to 1 mm of length.)

Solutions

Activity 1

Possible observations: No river is longer than 5000 miles. Each of the rivers is more than 2000 miles long and is probably longer than 2300 miles.

Solutions

Activity 2

1. The bars match the arrows in this order C, A, B, E, D.

2. Lengths are for C, A, B, E, D are 0.2 cm, 0.4cm, 0.6cm, 0.8cm, 0.9cm.

3. Some possibilites include 10 (4 + 6 or 2 + 8) 11, 13, 14, 17.

4. C, A, B, and D are worth about $3, $6, $9, and $14.

Extending the Activities

• •

- Have students place a different arrow on one of the number lines and explain relationships between their arrow and the other arrows.

- Have students create a number line with at least two benchmarks labeled and a few arrows. Ask them to draw some conclusions from their picture.

Picture It!

The lengths of the longest river in each of four continents are indicated on this number line. Describe some of the things this number line tells you.

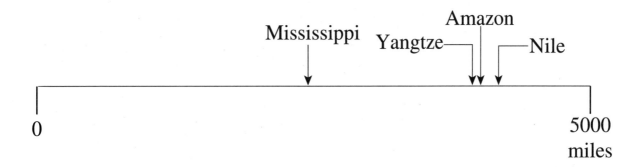

Here is a world map showing the four rivers. Where is each of the rivers located?

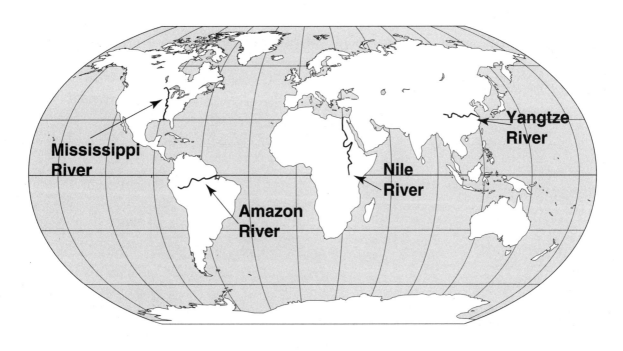

Picture It!

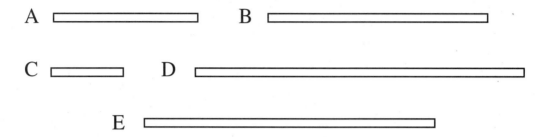

This is how a jeweler sees tiny bars of gold as he looks through a 10×
magnifying glass. He will use the bars to make different lengths in an
inlaid necklace.

1. Decide which bar would best match each arrow on the number line.

2. Estimate the approximate length of each bar.

3. Find four different lengths that could be made by combining rods.

4. If the gold in bar E is worth $12, about how much is each of the other
    bars worth.

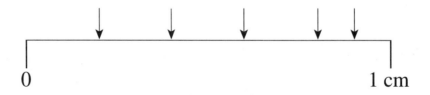

Under or Over?

Number Sense Focus

- Estimation
- Number relationships

Number Focus

- Activities 1–3: Whole numbers

Mathematical Background

• •

Many decisions about computational results can be made from estimates using only the lead digits of numbers, or using the lead digits and adjusting the estimation by examining the remaining digits. If something costs $10.67, the lead digits (10) tell us at a glance that the cost is over $10. Focusing on the lead digits sacrifices some accuracy but eliminates much messy computation. Research suggests that students often try to do exact computations and then "round" their results to produce an estimate. It is important that students realize that estimates are not exact computations, and that they become tolerant of error–a natural part of estimation.

Using the Activities

• •

In these activities, students experience the role that lead digits can play in making good estimates. Asking students to share their thinking and to explain their decision processes is an important focus of this activity. Encourage different techniques and explanations.

1. As a warm-up, write __ __ __ __ on the board. Ask students: What is the greatest number that can be written here? The smallest number? If you knew the first, or lead, digit was a 4, what could you say about the number? (It is at least 4000.) What is the greatest number it could be now? (4999)

2. In Activity 1, ask students to use estimation to help them decide which is the better estimate of each sum, and to explain how they decided. For

example: "In 536 + 329, 5 + 3 means 8 hundreds or 800. Since 36 and 29 are each less than 50, their sum is less than 100, so the sum must be less than 900." Make sure they realize that some values–such as 38 in problem 4–don't contribute much to the total.

3. Ask students to make similar decisions about the differences in Activity 2 and to explain their strategies. For example: "In 5263 – 1497, 5 – 1 means 4 thousands, or 4000. Since 263 is less than 497, a regrouping is required, so the difference is less than 4000."

4. Activity 3 is a bit more complicated. For part 1, one student might reason that "8759 + 7326 is about 15,000, and adding about 16,000 gives about 31,000, but subtracting 7000 would make the result under 30,000." Another student might reason that "7326 – 7195 is about zero, and 8759 + 15,937 is more than 20,000 but less than 30,000, so the result is under 30,000."

Solutions

Activity 1

1. under 900
2. over 10,000
3. over 70,000
4. under 1000
5. over 7000
6. under 90,000
7. No, it was under 30,000.

Activity 2

1. No, the club made less than $4000.
2. over 500
3. under 4000
4. over 50,000
5. under 300
6. over 5000
7. under 40,000

Activity 3

1. under 30,000
2. under 10,000
3. Washington School won the computer.

Extending the Activities

• Ask students to create a computation problem in which the lead digits are *not* sufficient to make an estimate.

• Ask students to make up a computation problem in which the result is between 50,000 and 60,000. Have them explain how they constructed their problem.

Under or Over?

Decide which is the better estimate, and explain your decision.

1. 536 + 329

   over 900
   under 900

2. 6387 + 7144

   over 10,000
   under 10,000

3. 65,743 + 8388

   over 70,000
   under 70,000

4. 665 + 38 + 229

   over 1000
   under 1000

5. 5349 + 492 + 1568

   over 7000
   under 7000

6. 71,736 + 5896 + 6376

   over 90,000
   under 90,000

RECORD ATTENDANCE!

Game 1	7,548 fans
Game 2	11,945 fans
Game 3	8,568 fans

7. Did the total attendance for the three-game series reach 30,000? Explain.

Under or Over?

Decide which is the better estimate, and explain your decision.

1. The Music Club made $4568 on their weekend car wash fund-raiser. Their expenses for the car wash were about $700. Did the club reach its goal? Explain.

2. 758 – 249

   over 500
   under 500

3. 5263 – 1497

   over 4000
   under 4000

4. 60,245 – 7897

   over 50,000
   under 50,000

5. 807 – 540

   over 300
   under 300

6. 7543 – 2489

   over 5000
   under 5000

7. 82,155 – 44,509

   over 40,000
   under 40,000

Under or Over?

Decide which is the better estimate, and explain your decision.

1. 8759 + 7326 + 15,937 – 7195

    over 30,000

    under 30,000

2. 15,864 – 5,938 + 26,888 – 27,217

    over 10,000

    under 10,000

BOOK DRIVE!

The books your school
collects will be donated to children
who need them—and you can
win a prize for the school library!

*Collect 2000 books and win
an encyclopedia!*

*Collect 3000 books and win a
computer with a CD-ROM drive!*

Sponsored by the Books for Children Club

3. The fifth graders at Washington School collected 975 books, the sixth graders collected 877 books, the seventh graders collected 758 books, and the eighth graders collected 487 books. Did Washington School win a prize? Explain.

EXPERIENCE 17

•••••••••••••••••••••••••••••••

Estimating Discounts

Number Sense Focus

- Estimation
- Number relationships

Number Focus

- Activities 1, 2: Percents, decimals
- Activity 3: Fractions, decimals

Mathematical Background

•••••••••••••••••••••••••••••••

Being able to identify compatible numbers is very helpful for estimating. For example, although discounts and discounted prices are not always easy to compute mentally, values can often be rounded to compatible numbers to make the computations easier. If an item that normally sells for $16.99 is on sale for $\frac{1}{3}$ off, the discount could be estimated by taking $\frac{1}{3}$ of $15, and $\frac{1}{3}$ of $18: the discount would be more than $5 and less than $6.

Using the Activities

•••••••••••••••••••••••••••••••

1. Display a game board. Go over the rules of the game, explaining that the game board contains *discounts* on items. Once the rules are understood, distribute a paper copy of the game to each pair.

2. As students play, remind them to identify the item and coupon they combined to compute each discount. As they share their choices, point out that different choices can produce the same discount. For example, 50% of $19.99 is about the same as 25% of $39.99.

Extending the Activities

•••••••••••••••••••••••••••••••

- Challenge pairs of students to create their own set of coupons, a list of items with prices, and a new game board.

- Ask students to make a new game board with discounted prices rather than discounts.

Estimating Discounts

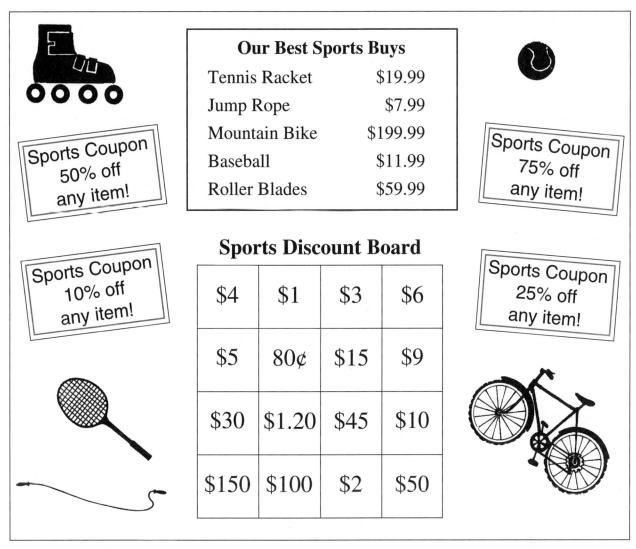

Our Best Sports Buys

Tennis Racket	$19.99
Jump Rope	$7.99
Mountain Bike	$199.99
Baseball	$11.99
Roller Blades	$59.99

Sports Coupon
50% off
any item!

Sports Coupon
75% off
any item!

Sports Coupon
10% off
any item!

Sports Coupon
25% off
any item!

Sports Discount Board

$4	$1	$3	$6
$5	80¢	$15	$9
$30	$1.20	$45	$10
$150	$100	$2	$50

Rules:

a. *The first of two players chooses an item and a coupon,* estimates *the discount, and places a marker on the estimated discount on the Sports Discount Board.*

b. *The other player verifies that the discount is correct and takes a turn, repeating the procedure.*

c. *To win get three discounts in a row—horizontally, vertically, or diagonally.*

Estimating Discounts

Computers and Peripherals

Keyboard	$59.99
Math Software	$29.95
Mouse	$88.88
Computer	$888.88
Color Monitor	$209.99

Computer Discount Board

$9	$89	$3	$21
$20	$70	$30	$222
$15	$10	$105	$444
$45	$6	$666	$66

Computer Coupon
10% off
any item!

Computer Coupon
50% off
any item!

Computer Coupon
33% off
any item!

Computer Coupon
75% off
any item!

Rules:

a. *The first of two players chooses an item and a coupon,* estimates *the discount, and places a marker on the estimated discount on the Computer Discount Board.*

b. *The other player verifies that the discount is correct and takes a turn, repeating the procedure.*

c. *To win get three discounts in a row—horizontally, vertically, or diagonally.*

Estimating Discounts

Exotic Fruits Discount Board

Exotic Fruit Coupon $\frac{1}{10}$ off any item!

$0.32	$0.80	$0.22	$0.60
$0.18	$1.06	$3.00	$0.45
$0.09	$1.60	$0.90	$0.44
$0.24	$1.20	$1.50	$2.00

Exotic Fruit Coupon $\frac{1}{4}$ off any item!

Exotic Fruit Coupon $\frac{1}{3}$ off any item!

Exotic Fruit Coupon $\frac{1}{2}$ off any item!

FURIUCHI FAMILY SINCE 1940
FRUITSTAND SPECIALS

PINEAPPLE $3.19   KIWI $0.88

MANGO $1.78   PAPAYA $2.39

DURIAN $5.99

Rules:

a. *The first of two players chooses an item and a coupon, estimates the discount, and places a marker on the estimated discount on the Exotic Fruits Discount Board.*

b. *The other player verifies that the discount is correct and takes a turn, repeating the procedure.*

c. *To win get three discounts in a row—horizontally, vertically, or diagonally.*

EXPERIENCE 18

Finding Compatible Fractions

Number Sense Focus

- Estimation
- Number relationships

Number Focus

- Activities 1–3: Fractions

Mathematical Background

Many fractions used and reported daily are not exact but are close enough to make meaningful interpretations. For example, about 29 million people live in California and about 260 million people live in the United States. However, $\frac{29}{260}$ is a difficult fraction to work with; $\frac{26}{260}$, or $\frac{1}{10}$, is much easier to handle. Since $\frac{26}{260}$ is less than $\frac{29}{260}$, the population of California about $\frac{1}{9}$ of the population of the United States. Just as compatible numbers are numbers that are easy to manipulate mentally, *compatible fractions* are fractions that are easy to work with and interpret mentally. *Near-compatible fractions*–compatible fractions that are near actual fractions–are often helpful for approximating and interpreting information.

Using the Activities

In these activities, students find and use compatible fractions, which will help them to look for relationships and to become more tolerant of inexactness.

1. Display the three fraction circles for Activity 1, and ask the first question. Ask: How are these fractions related? (They are equivalent, such as $\frac{1}{3} = \frac{2}{6} = \frac{12}{36}$.) Discuss the remaining questions.

2. Repeat the process for Activity 2. Circle C has been divided into 360 parts.

3. In Activity 3, ask students which fraction goes with which question and have them explain their choices. Or, mask the fractions, and have

students find their own compatible fractions. Either approach encourages students to think about important relationships among the fractions.

Solutions

Activity 1

1. $\frac{3}{4}$, $\frac{12}{16}$, $\frac{24}{32}$; They are equivalent fractions.

2. Possible answer: $\frac{13}{16}$, $\frac{26}{32}$

3. $\frac{1}{2}$; It is larger than both $\frac{5}{16}$ and $\frac{9}{32}$.

4. Possible answer: Circle C: $\frac{15}{32}$, $\frac{14}{32}$; Circle B: $\frac{7}{16}$, $\frac{6}{16}$

5. 64; Explanation: I continued the doubling pattern of 16, 32.

6. $\frac{48}{64}$

Activity 2

1. $\frac{2}{6}$, $\frac{12}{36}$, $\frac{120}{360}$; They are equivalent fractions, each equal to $\frac{1}{3}$.

2. Possible answer: $\frac{13}{36}$, $\frac{130}{360}$

3. $\frac{1}{6}$; It is much smaller than both $\frac{11}{36}$ and $\frac{119}{360}$.

4. Possible answer: Circle C: $\frac{179}{360}$, $\frac{177}{360}$; Circle B: $\frac{17}{36}$, $\frac{16}{36}$

5. Possible explanation: They are both 90.

Activity 3

1. $\frac{1}{6}$

2. $\frac{1}{5}$

3. $\frac{2}{3}$

4. $\frac{1}{1}$ or about the same

5. $\frac{1}{3}$

Extending the Activities

• •

- Ask students to name a fraction near but less than $\frac{1}{2}$; near but less than $\frac{75}{100}$; near but less than 1.

- Name a fraction such as $\frac{90}{365}$, and ask students for a real-world interpretation of the fraction (for example, this fraction might represent the part of the year completed by the end of March). Then name a near-fraction, such as $\frac{89}{365}$, and ask for an interpretation.

Finding Compatible Fractions

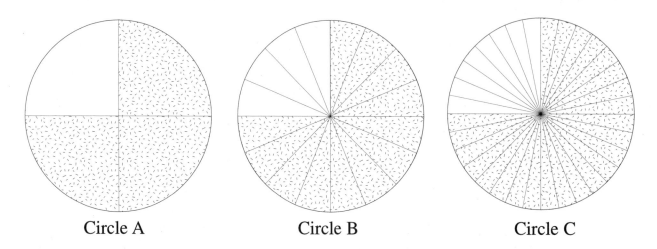

Circle A   Circle B   Circle C

1. For each circle, name the fraction shaded. What patterns or relationships do you see among the three fractions?

2. For Circle B, name a fraction that is a little larger than $\frac{3}{4}$. Name the equivalent fraction for Circle C.

3. For Circle A, name a fraction one section larger than $\frac{1}{4}$. How does it compare with a fraction one section larger than $\frac{1}{4}$ for Circle B? for Circle C?

4. For Circle C, name two fractions close to but less than $\frac{1}{2}$. Do the same for Circle B.

5. If you continued the pattern from Circle B to Circle C to another circle, Circle D, how many sections would it have? Explain how you decided.

6. What fraction in Circle D would be equivalent to the shaded area in the other circles?

Finding Compatible Fractions

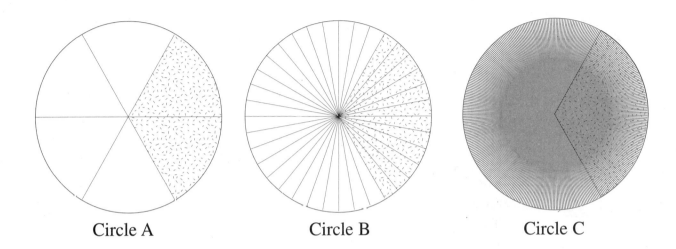

Circle A   Circle B   Circle C

1. For each circle, name the fraction shaded. What patterns or relationships do you see among the three fractions?

2. For Circle B, name a fraction that is a little larger than $\frac{1}{3}$. Name the equivalent fraction for Circle C, which is divided into 360°.

3. For Circle A, name a fraction one section smaller than $\frac{1}{3}$. How does it compare with a fraction one section smaller than $\frac{1}{3}$ for Circle B? For Circle C?

4. For Circle C, name two fractions close to but less than $\frac{1}{2}$. Do the same for Circle B.

5. How does the number of sections in a quarter of Circle C compare to the number of degrees in a right angle?

Finding Compatible Fractions

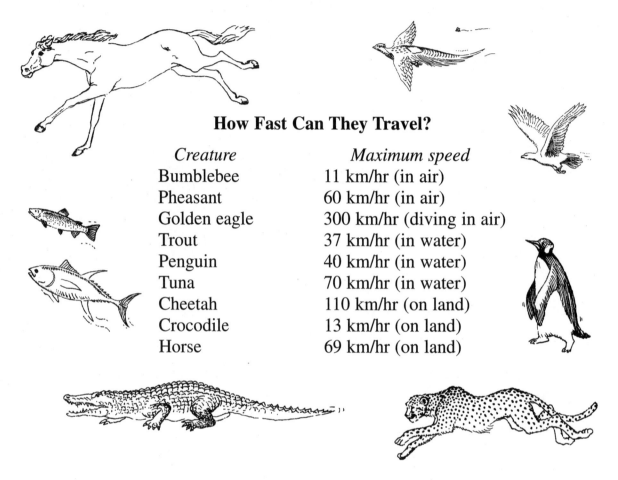

How Fast Can They Travel?

Creature	Maximum speed
Bumblebee	11 km/hr (in air)
Pheasant	60 km/hr (in air)
Golden eagle	300 km/hr (diving in air)
Trout	37 km/hr (in water)
Penguin	40 km/hr (in water)
Tuna	70 km/hr (in water)
Cheetah	110 km/hr (on land)
Crocodile	13 km/hr (on land)
Horse	69 km/hr (on land)

1. A bumblebee can fly about _____ the maximum speed of a horse.

2. A crocodile on land can reach about _____ the maximum speed of a horse.

3. A penguin can swim about _____ the maximum speed that a pheasant can fly.

4. A horse on land can travel about _____ the maximum speed of a tuna in water.

5. A cheetah can travel about _____ as fast as a diving golden eagle.

Match these answers with the blanks: $\frac{1}{6}$ $\frac{1}{3}$ $\frac{2}{3}$ $\frac{1}{1}$ $\frac{1}{5}$

Exploring Relative Size

An awareness of the relative size of numbers requires a knowledge of strategies for relating the sizes of numbers, but it also involves personal judgment and decision making. For example, is A.D. 1800 relatively recent? A scholar of ancient history would likely answer this question differently from a scholar of contemporary history. In terms of a human life span, 1980 is very recent to some people and ancient history to others. Clearly, personal knowledge, experience, and judgment are reflected in any decision about the relative size of numbers.

An understanding of the relative size of whole numbers and decimals depends on an understanding of place value. However, the relationships between whole numbers and decimals often result in confusion as students transfer experiences from one to the other. For example, place value quickly establishes that 4805 is larger than 980; yet, for decimals such as 0.9 and 0.4805, students often confuse the number of digits with their relative size. Strategies for comparing decimals include the technique of comparing them to critical benchmarks such as 0, 0.5, and 1.0.

Students also need practice with placing fractions in relation to other fractions. Strategies for comparing the sizes of fractions include understanding how fractions with equal numerators or denominators–such as $\frac{1}{5}$ and $\frac{1}{6}$, or $\frac{3}{7}$ and $\frac{4}{7}$ – are related, and an ability to compare fractions to critical benchmarks such as 0, $\frac{1}{2}$, and 1.

A feel for the relative size of numbers is important for making estimates. Depending on the circumstances, 1000, 900, 850, and 858 could all be good estimates for 857.6, because they are all relatively near the original value; however, 80, 90, 8000, and 9000 are unlikely to be reasonable estimates for 857.6, because they are relatively much smaller or larger.

The ability to move easily among fractions, decimals, and percents in making comparisons is often important. Suppose Tisha scored 34 out of 45 on her test. Is that good? Her brother scored 70%. How does that compare with Tisha's performance? Much worse? Slightly better? About the same? A person with good number sense does not usually need to do exact comparisons to answer such questions. For example, we could reason that Tisha's score is equivalent to 68 out of 90, and her brother scored only 2 points more out of a possible 100, which is enough of an estimate to make it clear that Tisha's is a relatively better score.

Sorting Fractions

Number Sense Focus

- Relative size
- Estimation
- Number relationships

Number Focus

- Activities 1–3: Fractions

Mathematical Background

Fractions take many different forms, and benchmarks are a useful starting point for thinking about the size of any fraction. The fraction benchmarks 0, $\frac{1}{2}$, and 1 are particularly helpful for estimating the size of many fractions. Recognizing relationships between numerators and denominators can help in identifying a fraction near a particular benchmark.

Using the Activities

1. As you use these activities, encourage students to look for patterns and use fraction benchmarks, and ask questions such as the following:

    - How can you recognize when a fraction is less than $\frac{1}{2}$ (or near a particular benchmark)?

    - What can you say about the numerator and denominator of these fractions?

    - Which fractions are the most difficult to sort? Why?

    - How can you think about the fraction $\frac{2}{19}$? What common fraction is it near?

2. As a warm-up, you might tell students your favorite fraction (any fraction will do). Write the fraction on the board. Make several statements about the fraction, and encourage students to add to the list. For example, suppose your fraction is $\frac{2}{5}$. Your list might be this:

- It is about $\frac{1}{2}$.
- It is the same as $\frac{4}{10}$.
- It is less than $\frac{1}{2}$.
- It is more than $\frac{1}{3}$.

3. Have students work in pairs. In Activity 1, they explore fractions near $\frac{1}{2}$. As pairs move the fraction cards around (self-stick notes work nicely), ask them to justify their placements to each other.

4. As students work on Activities 2 and 3, ask them to describe patterns related to the numerators, the denominators, and the size of the fractions.

Solutions

Activity 1

1. less than $\frac{1}{2}$: $\frac{9}{20}$, $\frac{7}{15}$, $\frac{14}{31}$; the others are greater than $\frac{1}{2}$
2. Their sum would be less than 1.

Activity 2

1. near 0: $\frac{1}{9}$, $\frac{2}{15}$, $\frac{7}{100}$, $\frac{2}{19}$, $\frac{3}{71}$; the others are near 1

3. Possible answer: $\frac{13}{15} + \frac{2}{15}$; (Sum of the numerators equals the denominator).
4. The sum would be near but less than 2.

Activity 3

1. near 0: $\frac{2}{19}$, $\frac{1}{6}$; near 1: $\frac{7}{9}$, $\frac{12}{15}$, $\frac{9}{10}$, $\frac{39}{40}$; the others are near $\frac{1}{2}$

2. near 0: $\frac{2}{19}$ is the smallest, $\frac{1}{6}$ is the largest; near $\frac{1}{2}$: $\frac{1}{3}$ is the smallest, $\frac{5}{8}$ is the largest; near 1: $\frac{7}{9}$ is the smallest, $\frac{39}{40}$ is the largest

3. $\frac{2}{19}$, $\frac{1}{6}$, $\frac{1}{3}$, $\frac{2}{5}$, $\frac{4}{7}$, $\frac{5}{8}$, $\frac{7}{9}$, $\frac{12}{15}$, $\frac{9}{10}$, $\frac{39}{40}$

Extending the Activities

• •

- Have students pair fraction cards so that the sum of the two fractions is close to 1.

- Ask students to choose a fraction card and decide what fraction would need to be added to it to make 1 (or to make $\frac{1}{2}$).

- After the fractions have been sorted, have students use a calculator to find their decimal equivalents. Discuss the patterns students see and how the decimal representation provides another sorting method.

Sorting Fractions

With your partner, make a set of fraction cards like these.

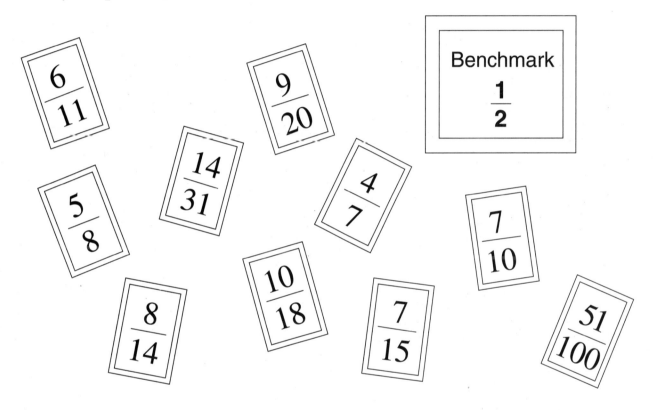

1. Sort your cards into two groups—fractions less than $\frac{1}{2}$ and fractions greater than $\frac{1}{2}$. Talk about your thinking with your partner.

2. If you were to choose any two fractions from the "less than $\frac{1}{2}$" pile, what could you say about their sum?

3. Make a new fraction card. Decide whether it is more or less than $\frac{1}{2}$, and explain why to your partner.

4. Make a new fraction card that is equivalent to but different from one of the fraction cards you already have.

Sorting Fractions

With your partner, make a set of fraction cards like these.

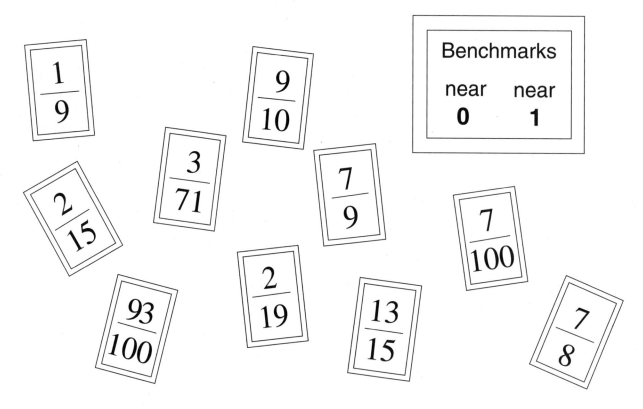

1. Sort your cards into two groups—fractions near 0 and fractions near 1. Talk about your thinking with your partner.

2. Make a new fraction card that is near 0 and another that is near 1. Explain your choices to your partner.

3. Find two fractions whose sum is 1. Tell your partner how you found them.

4. If you took any two fractions from the "near 1" pile, what could you say about their sum?

Sorting Fractions

With your partner, make a set of fraction cards like these.

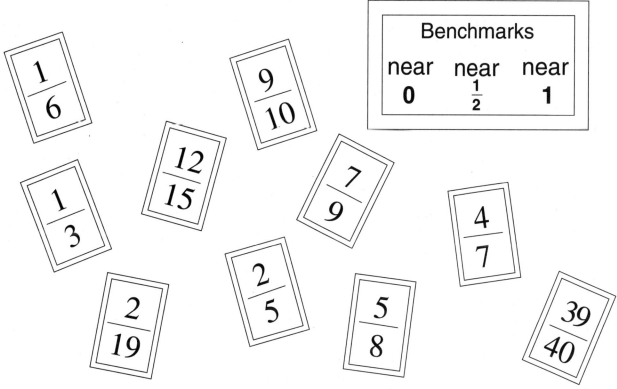

Benchmarks		
near **0**	near $\frac{1}{2}$	near **1**

1. Sort your cards into three groups—fractions near 0, fractions near $\frac{1}{2}$, and fractions near 1.

2. Within each group, decide which fraction is the largest and which is the smallest. Justify your thinking to your partner.

3. Order the fractions from least to greatest by estimating the size of each fraction.

4. Make a new fraction card. Add it to the set by placing it in the correct group.

5. Choose a fraction card. Make a new fraction card that, when added to the fraction you chose, makes 1.

EXPERIENCE 20

Sorting Decimals

Number Sense Focus

- Relative size
- Estimation

Number Focus

- Activities 1–3: Decimals

Mathematical Background

Recognizing that a decimal is near 0, less than 0.5, or near 1 is an important skill for ordering decimals and estimating decimal calculations. For example, recognizing that the sum of two decimals that are near but less than 0.5 must be less than 1, students can confidently estimate that a sum such as 0.446 + 0.48898 must be less than 1.

Using the Activities

These activities encourage the development and use of decimal benchmarks.

1. As students work, help them to explore patterns, and ask questions such as the following:
   - How can you recognize when a decimal is near a particular benchmark?
   - How do you know when a decimal is less than 0.5?
   - Are the number of decimal places important in determining the size of a decimal?
   - Why are decimals easier to order than fractions?
   - Which decimals are the most difficult to order? Why?

2. As a warm-up, ask students for some money amounts that are near but less than a half dollar (for example, $0.48, $0.45, and $0.49). Write the amounts in different forms (48¢, $0.48, $\frac{48}{100}$, 0.48). Students should realize that these are different representations of the same value.

3. Have students work in pairs on these activities. In Activity 1, each pair should make a set of decimal cards (self-stick notes work nicely). As pairs sort the decimal cards, ask them to justify their placements to each other. As you observe pairs working, ask them to describe, in general terms, how they know a decimal is more or less than the benchmark 0.5.

4. In Activity 2, ask pairs to describe how they know when a decimal is near the benchmark 0 or 1.

5. In Activity 3, students may struggle with question 4 after naming 0.52. Drawing a number line and renaming 0.51, 0.52, and 0.53 as 0.510, 0.520, and 0.530 may help stimulate discussion.

Solutions

Activity 1

1. less than 0.5: 0.46, 0.4444, 0.32, 0.48, 0.08; the others are greater than 0.5
4. Possible answer: 0.4444 is less than 0.5, which has fewer digits.
5. Their sum will be less than 1.

Activity 2

1. near 1: 0.98, 0.9, 0.95, 0.87, 0.921; the others are near 0
3. 0.98 and 0.02; 0.95 and 0.05
4. Their sum would be greater than 1 but less than 2.
5. No, because then you would have two decimals greater than 1/2, which would result in a sum greater than 1.

Activity 3

1. 0.53, 0.51, and 0.55
2. 0.49 and 0.51; 0.88 and 0.12

Extending the Activities

• •

- Ask students to pair decimal cards so that the sum of the two decimals is close to but less than 1 (or more than 1).

- Put all the decimal cards in a bowl (add new ones if you like), and have students draw out two at a time, tell which decimal is larger, and explain why.

Sorting Decimals

With your partner, make a set of decimal cards like these.

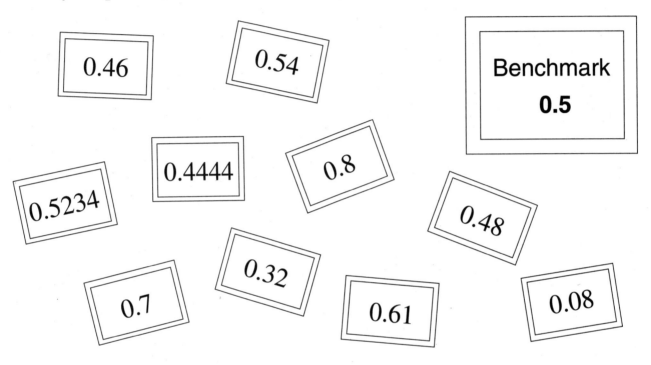

1. Sort your cards into two groups—decimals less than 0.5 and decimals greater than 0.5. Justify your thinking to your partner.

2. Make a new decimal card. Decide whether it is more or less than 0.5, and explain why to your partner.

3. Make a new decimal card that is equivalent to but different from one of the decimal cards you already have.

4. Find a decimal that proves this statement: "The magnitude, or relative size, of a decimal is not determined by the number of digits it has."

5. If you took any two decimals from the "less than 0.5" pile, what could you say about their sum?

Sorting Decimals

With your partner, make a set of decimal cards like these.

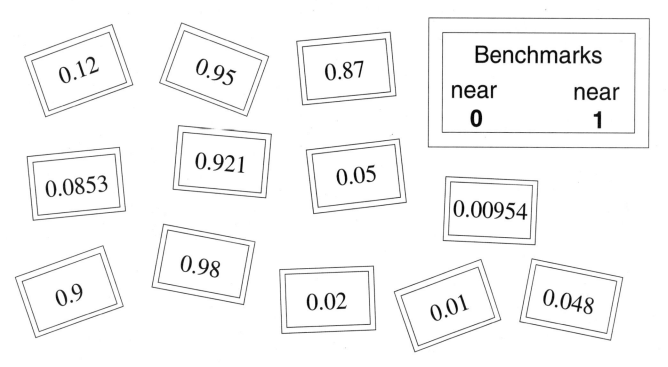

1. Sort your cards into two groups—decimals near 0 and decimals near 1. Justify your thinking to your partner.

2. Make a new decimal card that is near 0 and another that is near 1.

3. Find two decimals whose sum is 1.

4. If you took any two decimals from the "near 1" pile, what could you say about their sum?

5. Choose a decimal card. Make a new decimal card with a decimal greater than the decimal on the card you chose and so, if you add the decimals together, you get exactly 1. Can you choose a decimal card of more than 0.5 for this problem? Why or why not?

Sorting Decimals

With your partner, make a set of decimal cards like these.

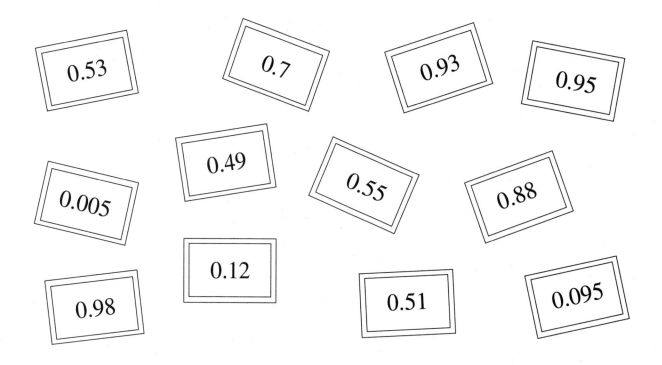

1. Find three decimals between $\frac{1}{2}$ and $\frac{6}{10}$.

2. Find two decimal cards whose sum is exactly 1.

3. Find two decimal cards whose sum is almost 1.

4. Make two new decimal cards that are between 0.51 and 0.53.

5. Make two new decimal cards so that their sum is more than 0.5 but less than 1.

....

Which Is Bigger?

Number Sense Focus

• Relative size

Number Focus

• Activity 1: Whole numbers
• Activity 2: Decimals

Mathematical Background

....

An awareness of the relative size of numbers requires an understanding of place value and multiple representation and, for decimals, the concept of decimals as well as decimal place value and relevant vocabulary. These activities employ a variety of representations to help students explore and develop confidence with the concept of relative sizes of whole numbers and decimals.

Using the Activities

....

1. Activity 1 introduces different ways to name and represent whole numbers. Show the top half of the transparency, and invite students to choose two numbers to compare. Allow them time to prepare their explanations, and encourage discussion. Some students have made the following comparisons:

   • "I chose 1000 and 100 thousand. Since 100 thousand is 100×1000, it is greater."

   • "I chose 10^4 and 400,000. Since 10^4 is 10,000, 400,000 is greater."

   Encourage other students to comment on the explanations and to suggest other ways of reasoning.

2. Use Activity 2 and the bottom half of Activity 1 in the same way.

Extending the Activities

- Challenge students to decide which pair of numbers in a set is closest together and to explain why.

- Invite pairs of students to arrange all the numbers from least to greatest. Then, challenge them to find a number that fits between each successive pair of numbers.

- Invite students to suggest real-world examples of each number.

Which Is Bigger?

Choose two of these numbers, decide which is greater, and explain your decision.

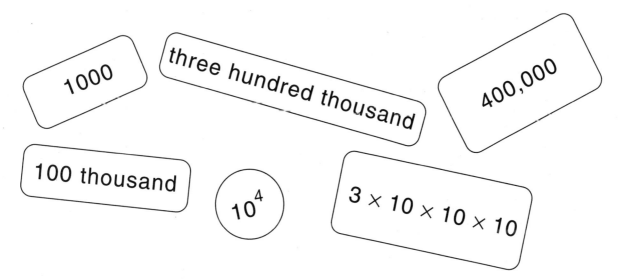

Choose two of these numbers, decide which is greater, and explain your decision.

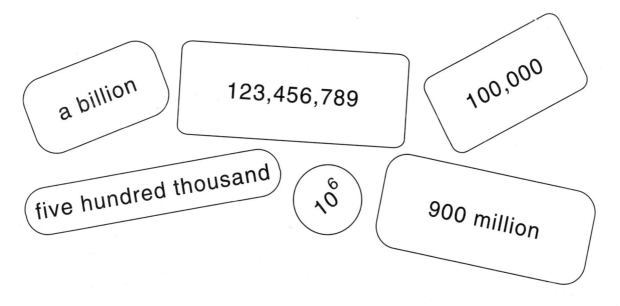

Which Is Bigger?

Choose two of these numbers, decide which is greater, and explain your decision.

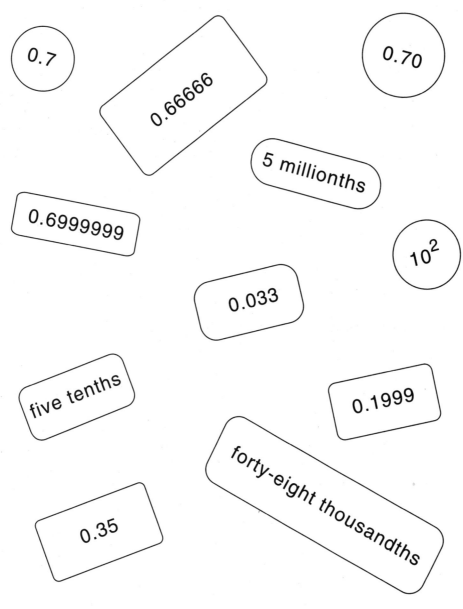

Number SENSE / Grades 4–6

More Which Is Bigger?

Number Sense Focus

- Relative size

Number Focus

- Activity 1: Fractions
- Activity 2: Fractions, percents
- Activity 3: Fractions, percents, decimals

Mathematical Background

The ability to move freely among symbolic representations of the same number—for example, fraction, decimal, and percent representations—is another important number sense skill. Comparing fractions is sometimes easier if the decimal or percent approximations are known or easily computed mentally.

Using the Activities

1. Activity 1 is a simple introductory activity to build confidence and encourage discussion. The fractions are common, and their relative size should be recognized. Show the transparency, and invite students to choose two numbers to compare. Allow them time to prepare their explanations. Students have made these comparisons:

   - "I chose $\frac{1}{6}$ and $\frac{5}{6}$. I know $\frac{5}{6}$ is greater, because it takes five $\frac{1}{6}$'s to equal $\frac{5}{6}$."

   - "I chose $\frac{3}{8}$ and $\frac{2}{3}$. I know $\frac{2}{3}$ must be greater, because it is more than $\frac{1}{2}$, and $\frac{3}{8}$ is less than $\frac{1}{2}$."

   Encourage other students to comment on the explanations and to suggest other ways of reasoning.

2. Use Activity 2 in the same way. The fractions in Activity 2 are frequently used and can be connected to common decimal equivalents.

3. Activity 3 entails more challenging comparisons, as fractions, percents, and decimals are presented. However, there are some simple pairs that can be chosen by less confident students. In Activity 3, students have made these comparisons:

- "I chose $\frac{3}{10}$ and 0.4, and 0.4 is greater because $\frac{3}{10}$ is the same as 0.3."

- "I choose 27% and $\frac{1}{4}$. I know 27% is greater, because I changed $\frac{1}{4}$ to 25 hundredths, which is 25%."

Extending the Activities

- Challenge students to decide which pair of numbers in a set is the closest together and to explain why.

- Invite pairs of students to arrange all the numbers from least to greatest. Then, challenge them to find a number that fits between each pair of successive numbers.

- Invite students to represent some of the numbers with drawings or diagrams.

- Ask students for fraction, decimal, or percent equivalents for all of the numbers.

More Which Is Bigger?

Choose two of these numbers, decide which is greater, and explain your decision.

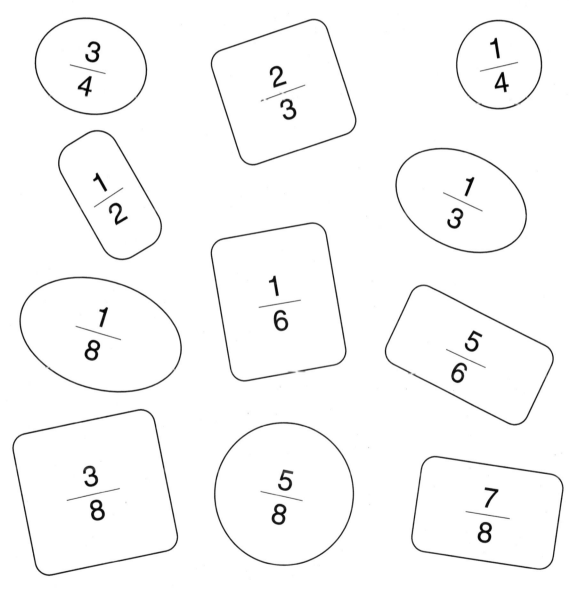

More Which Is Bigger?

Choose two of these numbers, decide which is greater, and explain your decision.

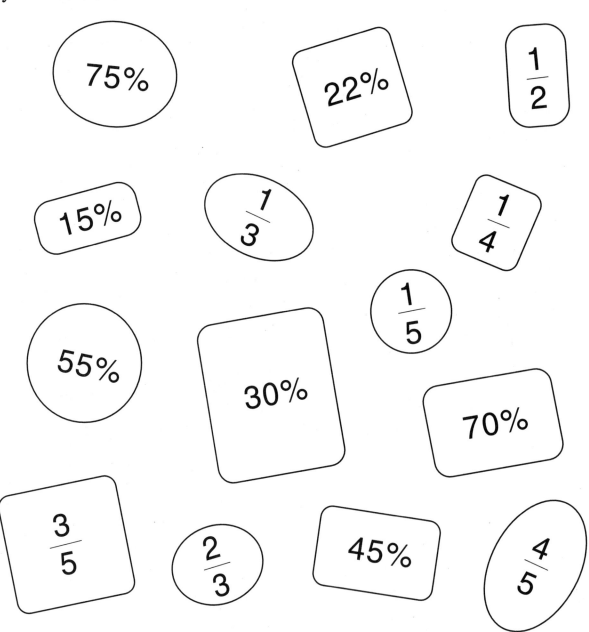

More Which Is Bigger?

Choose two of these numbers, decide which is greater, and explain your decision.

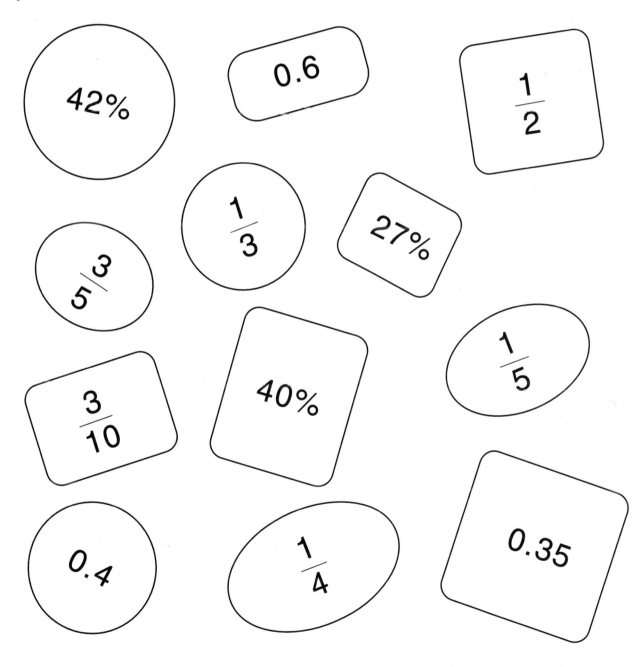

EXPERIENCE 23

Where Is It?

Number Sense Focus

- Relative size
- Estimation

Number Focus

- Activity 1: Whole numbers, fractions, decimals

Mathematical Background

Scales or subdivisions along a number line provide important clues for locating numbers. Recognizing the range of values for an interval of a number line is the first step. For example, if the end points of the interval are labeled 0 and 1000, then every point along the interval must be greater than 0 and less than 1000. Locating the midpoint of the interval establishes the location of 500; locating the midpoint of each of the two new sections locates 250 and 750. Such subdivisions are helpful for estimating the values of intermediate points.

Using the Activity

This activity encourages students to use the idea of subdividing a number line into intervals to estimate values along the line.

1. Show the unmarked number line on the top of the transparency, and label the end points 0 and 100. Ask students to identify the midpoint (the halfway point); to show about where 90 is located (near 100); to show about where 45 is located (near but to the left of the midpoint); and to show about where 10 is located (near but to the right of 0). Now point to several locations, one at a time, and ask students to name the number near each point.

2. Change the end points to other values (such as 0 and 1000; 500 and 600; 0 and 1; 0.7 and 0.9; or $1\frac{1}{2}$ and $2\frac{1}{2}$). Ask students to identify the

midpoint and then to estimate the value of other points on the new number line.

3. Have students work in groups. Ask each group to draw a number line and label the end points of an interval. Have them find the midpoint and explain how they did it. Then, ask students to take turns placing their pencil on the number line and asking another person in the group to estimate the location of the point and tell how he or she decided.

4. Show the number line on the bottom of the transparency, and label the end points (for example, 0 and 100). Ask questions, such as:

   • Is B more than 50 or less than 50?

   • What letter is near 100? Near 0?

   • If C is 22, where would 20 likely be?

5. For a particular set of end points, explore general questions regarding the labels, such as these:

   • What two values added together about equal D? Explain. (B and E, because B is a little less than half of D, and E is a little more than half of D.)

   • Is $A + C > E$, or is $A + C < E$? Explain. ($A + C < E$, because A and C are each less than half of E.)

   • Is $E \div B > 1$, or is $E \div B < 1$? Explain. ($E \div B > 1$, because E is greater than B.)

   • Is $E \div C < E \div A$? Explain. (Yes, because A is smaller than C, so $E \div A$ would produce the greater quotient.)

   Help students realize that all of these questions would be answered the same regardless of the values assigned to the end points.

Extending the Activity

• •

   • Have students draw a number line and label the midpoint, decide on labels for the end points, and label several other points on the line.

   • Have students draw an arc of a circle, decide on labels for the end points, then estimate and label other points on the arc.

Where Is It?

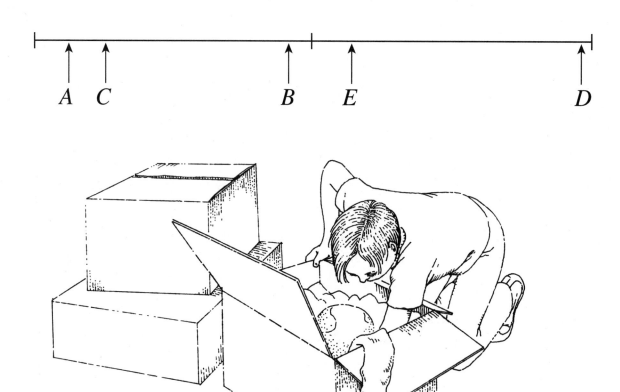

A   C   B   E   D

· ·

Where Are You?

Number Sense Focus

- Relative size
- Estimation

Number Focus

- Activities 1–3: Fractions

Mathematical Background

· ·

A region that has been subdivided offers visual clues for the naming of fractions. Recognizing $\frac{1}{4}$, for example, is made easier by dividing a two-dimensional, regular shape into quarters or a number line into fourths.

Using the Activities

· ·

These activities provide one model for encouraging students to estimate the relative size of fractions.

1. For each activity, show the transparency, and ask questions that focus students' attention on the shape.

   - How many sides does this polygon have?

   - Are all the sides the same length? (Yes; each figure is equilateral.)

   - Are all the angles congruent? (Yes; each figure is equiangular.)

2. Make sure students recognize the relationship between the sides of each figure and the fractional parts represented. In Activity 1, $\frac{2}{5}$ represents two complete sides of the pentagon. In Activity 2, $\frac{2}{6}$ represents two complete sides of the hexagon.

3. Have students work in groups to draw each polygon and to share their results as the questions on the transparency are discussed. For question 5, walk around the room and check where they have placed their finger on the polygon and how they have named that position.

4. Ask questions that encourage students to find other positions on the regular polygons and also to estimate fractions between the vertices.

Solutions

Activity 1

1. on vertex C
2. Answers will vary. Encourage students to focus on the relationship that distance traveled + distance remaining = 1. If you have gone $\frac{2}{5}$, you have $\frac{3}{5}$ farther to go.
3. between B and C (which can be expressed symbolically as $\frac{1}{5} < \frac{1}{4} < \frac{2}{5}$)
4. between A and B, so $0 < \frac{1}{6} < \frac{1}{5}$

Activity 2

1. on vertex F
2. Answers will vary. Encourage students to focus on the relationship that distance traveled + distance remaining = 1.
3. on vertex D (which can be expressed as $\frac{1}{2} = \frac{3}{6}$)
4. between B and C (which can be expressed as $\frac{1}{6} < \frac{1}{4} < \frac{2}{6}$)

Activity 3

1. on vertex D
2. Answers will vary. Encourage students to focus on the relationship that distance traveled + distance remaining = 1.
3. on vertex J; $\frac{9}{10}$ is the same as 0.9.
4. between D and E (which can be expressed as $\frac{3}{10} < \frac{1}{3} < \frac{4}{10}$)

Extending the Activities

- Have students estimate fractions–represented as positions on regular polygons–near the familiar benchmark of $\frac{1}{2}$.

- Have students estimate the position of other non–unit fractions, such as $\frac{2}{3}$ and $\frac{3}{4}$.

- Challenge students to make other regular polygons and estimate different positions around them.

- As a class, map out a hiking expedition with campsites, rest areas, and places of interest, and decide what site you would be near n way through the trip, where n takes on different fractional values.

Where Are You?

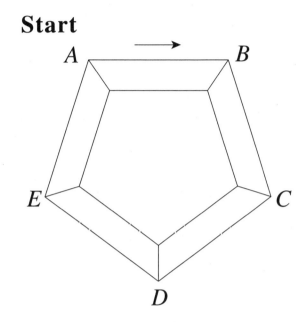

Start

Before each question, begin at the vertex marked **Start**.

1. Where will you be when you have gone $\frac{2}{5}$ of the way around the pentagon?

2. Place your finger on a vertex. What fraction of the distance have you gone when you have reached that vertex? How much farther do you have to go to make a complete trip around the pentagon?

3. About where would you be if you went $\frac{1}{4}$ of the distance around the pentagon?

4. About where would you be if you went $\frac{1}{6}$ of the distance around the pentagon?

5. Place your finger on the pentagon (but not on a vertex), and estimate the fraction of the distance you have traveled to that point.

Where Are You?

Start

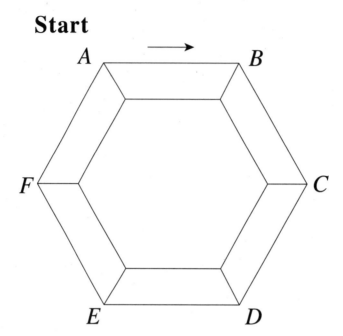

Before each question, begin at the vertex marked **Start.**

1. Where will you be when you have gone $\frac{5}{6}$ of the way around the hexagon?

2. Place your finger on a vertex. How far will you have gone when you reach that vertex? How much farther do you have to go to make a complete trip around the hexagon?

3. About where would you be if you went $\frac{1}{2}$ of the distance around the hexagon?

4. About where would you be if you went $\frac{1}{4}$ of the distance around the hexagon?

5. Place your finger on the hexagon (but not on a vertex), and estimate the fraction of the distance you have traveled to that point.

Where Are You?

Start

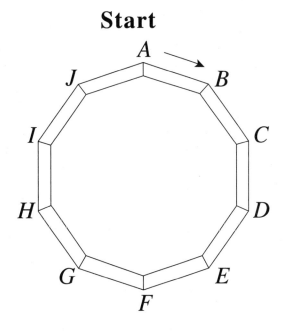

1. Where will you be when you have gone $\frac{3}{10}$ of the way around the decagon?

2. Place your finger on a vertex. How far will you have gone when you reach that vertex? How much farther do you have to go to make a complete trip around the decagon?

3. About where would you be if you went $\frac{9}{10}$ of the distance around the decagon? How would you name this as a decimal?

4. About where would you be if you went $\frac{1}{3}$ of the distance around the decagon?

5. Place your finger on the decagon (but not on a vertex), and estimate the fraction of the distance you have traveled to that point.

EXPERIENCE 25

• •

Time Out

Number Sense Focus

- Relative size
- Multiple representation
- Reasonableness

Number Focus

- Activities 1–3: Whole numbers

Mathematical Background

• •

Concepts involving units of time—seconds, minutes, hours, days, weeks, fortnights, months, years, leap years, decades, centuries, and millennia—are developed slowly. Some of these units make useful benchmarks, and each is related to the others by patterns and numerical equivalents. Units of time sometimes offer historical connections. For example, *septennial* means occurring every 7 years, and *septuagenarian* is a person in his or her seventies; *sept* is a combining form meaning seven. This naturally raises the question of why September is the ninth rather than the seventh month. Historically, the Roman calendar had March as the first month, thus September was the seventh month.

Using the Activities

• •

In these activities, students explore different units of time. Calculators can help with finding exact values, but encourage students to evaluate whether their results are reasonable.

1. Students often measure time by their personal benchmarks, such as their grade, their birthday, and special or disturbing events. For example, "Did it happen before my birth or after my birth?" As a warm-up, ask students to share their personal benchmarks. You might also talk about calendars, which provide a way to review larger units of time such as weeks, months, and years. We generally connect 365 days to a year, with a leap

year every 4 years. You might mention that a year is really closer to $365\frac{1}{4}$ days, which is why every 4 years we "catch up" with a leap year. A leap year occurs in every year that can be divided by 4 evenly, except for the years that mark the hundreds—such as 1500, 1600, and 1700—which are leap years only if they can be divided by 400.

2. Some words for measuring time may be unfamiliar to students; you may want to discuss them. For example, *fortnight,* meaning two weeks, is commonly used in England, and *score* means 20. The word *millennium* may not be familiar to students, but as the twenty-first century approaches, it will be used more frequently.

3. Talk about decades and centuries. Decades are 10-year spans—from, say, 1980 to 1989 or 2000 to 2009. Centuries are 100-year spans—from, 1901 to 2000 (the twentieth century) or 2001 to 2100 (the twenty-first century). The year 2001 also marks the beginning of a millennium.

4. Conduct each activity by displaying the transparency and discussing the questions. You might choose to cover the words used for the fill-in-the-blank questions.

Solutions

Activity 1

1. yes; $60 \times 24 = 1440$ minutes
2. no; $24 \times 31 = 744$ hours at the most
3. minutes in a month, since $60 \times 24 \times 31$ is greater than 24×365
4. days in a month, as 28 is greater than $365 \div 14$
5. day
6. fortnight
7. week
8. year

Activity 2

1. Tuesday
2. Wednesday
3. 1904, 1908, 1912, 1916, 1920
4. 2000
5. 3; yes; 1920, 1924, 1928 and 1960, 1964, 1968
6. 2004, 2008, 2012, 2016, 2020

Activity 3

1. bicentennial
2. septuagenarian
3. fortnight
4. annual
5. millennium
6. decade
7. century
8. centennial

Extending the Activities

- Have students research and report when and why our current calendar came into existence.

- Have students identify different New Year's holidays (such as Chinese New Year) or report on different ways of reporting the years (Japan, for example, reports the year of the reign of their emperor).

- Ask about *octogenarian, octopus,* and *October.* What do they have in common? Why is our tenth month October?

- When President Lincoln said, "Four score and seven years ago," how many years ago did he mean? How else could he have said this?

- Have students find the number of days they have lived.

Time Out

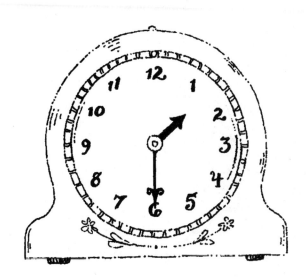

1. Are there more than 1000 minutes in a day?

2. Are there more than 1000 hours in a month?

3. Are there more hours in a year or more minutes in a month?

4. Are there more days in a month or more fortnights in a year?

In 5—8, decide which of these terms will make the statement reasonable:

day **year** **fortnight** **week**

5. A _____ has fewer than 1500 minutes.

6. A _____ is 2 weeks.

7. A _____ is 168 hours.

8. A _____ has about $365\frac{1}{4}$ days.

Time Out

1. If New Year's Day falls on Monday of a non—leap year, what day of the week is the next New Year's Day?

2. If New Year's Day falls on Monday of a leap year, what day of the week is the next New Year's Day?

3. What were the first five leap years of the twentieth century?

4. What is the last leap year of the twentieth century?

5. What are the most leap years that could occur in any decade? Did this number of leap years occur in any decades of the twentieth century? If so, name one or two.

6. What will be the first five leap years of the twenty-first century?

7. What will the date be one year from today? One decade from today?

8. What year will it be one century from today? One millennium from today?

Time Out

Decide which of these terms will make each statement reasonable:

decade   **centennial**   **bicentennial**   **fortnight**

millennium   **annual**   **septuagenarian**   **century**

1. In 1976 the United States celebrated its _____ .

2. Ronald Reagan was a(n) _____ when he was elected president.

3. The Wimbledon tennis tournament lasts a(n) _____ .

4. There is a(n) _____ holiday to commemorate the birthday of Dr. Martin Luther King Jr.

5. The year 2001 begins a new century and a new _____ .

6. Every _____ has two or three leap years.

7. Students in school today will live most of their lives in the twenty-first _____ .

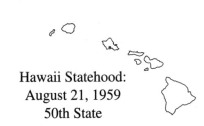

Hawaii Statehood:
August 21, 1959
50th State

Alaska Statehood:
January 3, 1959
49th State

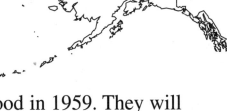

8. Alaska and Hawaii were granted statehood in 1959. They will celebrate their statehood _____ in 2059.

Exploring Multiple Representation

Numbers may be expressed in a variety of symbolic and graphical representations. For example:

- $\frac{3}{4}$ is equivalent to $\frac{6}{8}$ and 0.75 and 75%.

- 30 cents is 3 dimes or a quarter plus a nickel.

- 30 minutes is a $\frac{1}{2}$ hour.

- The fraction *one half* may be expressed by its word name, the symbol $\frac{1}{2}$, or a drawing:

- The expression $\frac{1}{2} + \frac{1}{2} + \frac{1}{2} + \frac{1}{2}$ is the same as $4 \times \frac{1}{2}$. (Recognizing the connection between addition and multiplication can help a student better understand fraction–whole number relationships.)

Understanding multiple representation, recognizing that some representations are more useful than others in certain problem-solving situations, and being able to generate equivalent representations are essential number sense skills.

For example, suppose a person is checking out at the market and has a bill of $8.53. The person could pay with a $10 bill and get $1.47 change. However, if the customer wanted to carry fewer coins, he or she could pay with a $10 bill and 3 pennies, and receive change of $1.50. Decomposing $8.53 into $8.50 + $0.03 provides the rationale.

Activities in this section promote several ways to think about equivalent forms of numbers. Experiences in thoughtfully breaking numbers apart–decomposing–and putting them together–recomposing–in different but equivalent ways develop a useful skill. The ability to recognize and create numerical representations that simplify problems is an indication of high-level mathematical thinking.

....

Calculating Differently

Number Sense Focus

- Multiple representation
- Mental computation

Number Focus

- Activity 1: Whole numbers

Mathematical Background

....

Thinking about different ways to represent a number stimulates creative thinking and provides an interesting context in which to practice basic facts while applying important operation and number relationships. This activity may also stimulate a discussion of the order of operations–including notation such as parentheses, used to indicate order.

Using the Activity

....

Every student or pair of students should have a four-function calculator available for this activity.

1. As a warm-up, indicate a Start Number, 8, and a Goal Number, 16. If you have an overhead calculator, show an 8 in the display. Ask students what operations they could perform to move from 8 to 16. For example:

   $8 + 8 = 16$ $8 \times 4 \div 2 = 16$ $8 + 2 + 2 + 2 + 2 = 16$

   $8 \times 2 = 16$ $8 \div 0.5 = 16$ $(8 - 4) \times 4 = 16$

   You might state this ground rule: You must begin with the Start Number and, without clearing your calculator, end up with the Goal Number.

2. Show the transparency, and ask students to make a list of the different ways they can get 240 from the Start Number, 8. Remind them to record their key strokes or the operations they perform. As they work, ask them

to copy their solutions onto the board–making sure no other student has already recorded that method on the board. This will result in a class list of methods that all students can see and discuss.

Solutions

Here are some ways students have done this problem:

$8 \times 30 = 240$ $\qquad$ $8 \times 3 \times 10 = 240$

$8 \times 100 - 560 = 240$ $\qquad$ $(8 - 7) \times 240 = 240$

$8 \times 6 \times 5 = 240$ $\qquad$ $8 \div 8 \times 240 = 240$

$8 \times 50 - 160 = 240$ $\qquad$ $8 \times 60 \div 2 = 240$

$8 \div 2 \times 60 = 240$ $\qquad$ $8 \div 4 \times 120 = 240$

$8 + 232 = 240$ $\qquad$ $8 + 8 + 8 + 8 + \ldots + 8 = 240$

Extending the Activity

- Present other Start Numbers and Goal Numbers.

- Present other Start Numbers and Goal Numbers, and require that certain other numbers be used. For example: The Start Number is 25, the Goal Number is 100, and you must use a 10 at least once. (Thus, $25 \times 4 = 100$ is not a legitimate solution; $25 + 10 + 65 = 100$ and $25 \div 10 \times 40 = 100$ are.)

Calculating Differently

Make a list of the ways you can start with the Start Number and get the Goal Number.

Start Number ☐   Goal Number ☐

EXPERIENCE 27

• •

How Could It Happen?

Number Sense Focus

- Multiple representation
- Mental computation

Number Focus

- Activities 1–3: Whole numbers

Mathematical Background

• •

These activities offer students additional practice in generating equivalent relationships.

Using the Activities

• •

1. As a warm-up, ask students for different ways to make 10, such as 5×2, $60 \div 6$, $6 + 4$, and $\frac{1}{2}$ of 20. Create a list of their suggestions.

2. In Activity 1, make sure students understand the rule for operating on numbers. Make a list of the different solutions that are proposed for each question, and discuss how each was found. You may want to have students search for all the possible answers to each question.

3. In Activities 2 and 3, encourage students to explain their thinking as they answer the questions.

Solutions

Activity 1

1. Possible answers: $3 + 12$, $6 + 9$, $7 + 8$, $8 + 7$, $10 + 5$, $14 + 1$, 3×5, 15×1
2. 10×5
3. Some possible answers: 3×7, 3×9, 6×4, 10×2, 22×1, 14×2, $8 + 12$, $14 + 12$, $15 + 9$
4. 264, by multiplying 12 and 22
5. Possible answers: 1, 2, 25, 33, 37, 38, 39, 41, 43, 45, 46, 47

Activity 2

1. $100 \times 100 = 10{,}000$
2. Possible answers: $100 + 100$, 100×2, 20×10, 40×5
3. 700
4. 87

Activity 3

1. largest: $60 \times 1000 = 60{,}000$; smallest: $0 \times$ any other number $= 0$
2. Possible answers: 10×200; 40×50
3. 3600
4. 10

Extending the Activities

- Change the rules to subtraction and division, and have students explore the implications for each question.

- Suggest that students make up mysteries. For example, in Activity 1, Barbara chose two numbers and an operation and got 24. She said that if she used the other operation on her numbers, the result would be on the first spinner. What could her numbers be?

How Could It Happen?

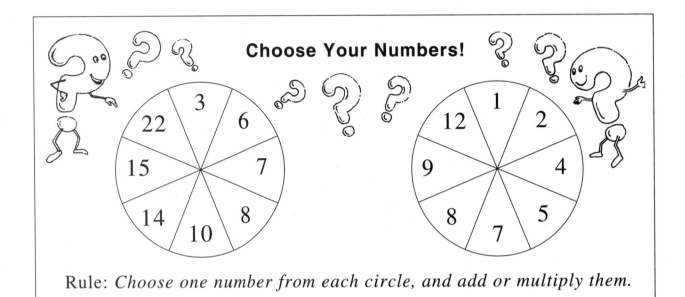

Choose Your Numbers!

Rule: *Choose one number from each circle, and add or multiply them.*

1. Alex chose two numbers and got 15. What number did he pick from each circle?

2. Ben chose two numbers and got 50. What numbers did he choose?

3. Sook Leng got a result in the twenties. What numbers could she have chosen?

4. Shamariah got the largest result possible. What did she get, and how did she get it?

5. Chalise named a number less than 50 that could not be made using the rules. What number did she name?

How Could It Happen?

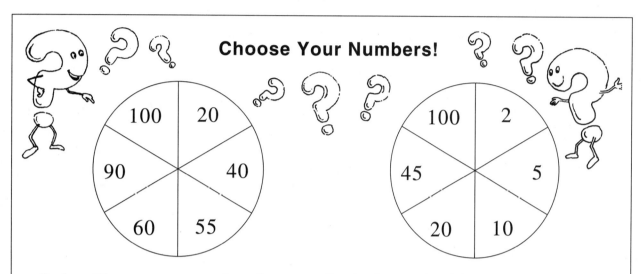

Choose Your Numbers!

Circle 1: 100 20 90 40 60 55

Circle 2: 100 2 45 5 20 10

Rule: *Choose one number from each circle, and add or multiply them.*

1. What numbers and operation could be chosen to make the largest number?

2. What numbers and operation could be chosen to make 200?

3. Which of these numbers cannot be made?

    300   400   550   700   1800

4. Which of these numbers cannot be made?

    22   60   87   135   275

5. Choose a number from each circle and an operation. Tell your result to a partner, and keep track of how many guesses it takes your partner to find your numbers.

How Could It Happen?

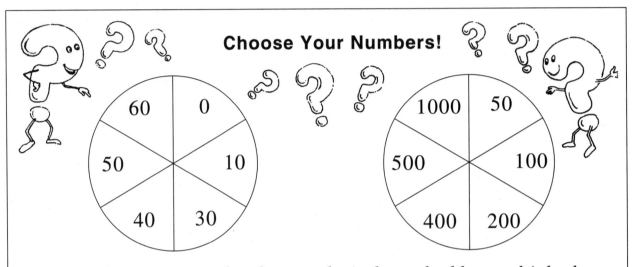

Choose Your Numbers!

60   0
50   10
40   30

1000   50
500   100
400   200

Rule: *Choose one number from each circle, and add or multiply them.*

1. What numbers and operation would make the largest number? The smallest number?

2. What numbers and operation could be used to make 2000?

3. Which of these numbers cannot be made?

   3000   3600   4000   5000   6000

4. Which of these numbers cannot be made?

   0   10   60   410   560   6000

5. Choose a number from each circle and an operation. Tell your result to a partner, and keep track of how many guesses it takes your partner to find your numbers.

Every Graph Tells a Story

Number Sense Focus

- Multiple representation

Number Focus

- Activities 1–3: Whole numbers, fractions, percents

Mathematical Background

The ability to make sense of quantitative data presented in graphical form is an important element of number sense. Students need to feel comfortable inferring information from the shape, the relative size of columns, and the pattern of data points in graphical displays.

Using the Activities

In these activities, students are presented with graphs and asked to invent situations that they could describe. The emphasis is on realistically interpreting the quantitative information presented.

1. Show the first graph in Activity 1. Explain that the graph is showing some information, but as no title and no labels are given, we cannot tell what the graph is about. Invite students to invent a story that would fit the graph. Emphasize that the story should contain numbers appropriate for the graph. Here are two explanations students have created for this graph:

   - "The graph is about the baskets we shot. I shot 4–that's me on the left–James shot 2, and Kai shot 3."

   - "The graph shows how much money we have saved. Sandy has $80, I've only got $40, and Juli has $60."

2. Show each of the other graphs in turn, and ask for stories to fit them. Encourage discussion about the extent to which each story fits the graph and is realistic.

3. Conduct Activities 2 and 3 in the same way.

Solutions

Stories will vary; one possible scenario is presented for each graph.

Activity 1

2. This shows the cost for stamps. Eight $1 stamps cost $8, seven cost $7, six cost $6, five cost $5, and four cost $4.

3. On Water Street, all the traffic lights have a red and a green light, and $\frac{1}{10}$ of the traffic lights have a yellow light too.

4. I spent over $2\frac{1}{2}$ hours playing on Monday and almost 4 hours on Tuesday. On Wednesday I had a little over 4 hours to play because I didn't have any homework. Thursday I played for $3\frac{1}{2}$ hours, and on Friday I played for 5 hours because there's no school on Saturday.

5. Each committee had a different number of volunteers. Committees I and IV had three volunteers, Committee II had four volunteers, and Committee III had two volunteers.

6. Eight people started a 4-mile walk. Every mile, two people dropped out. Only two people finished the walk.

Activity 2

1. The left circle represents students who have birds as pets, and the right circle represents students who have dogs. *B* and *S* have birds, *N* has a dog, *J* has a bird and a dog, and *T* has neither pet.
2. The left circle contains numbers divisible by 3, and the right circle contains numbers divisible by 2.
3. Figures with four sides are inside the circle. Figures with other numbers of sides are outside the circle.
4. I was going downhill on my bike. I got up to 15 mph. Then I slowed down because I was going up a hill but sped up again when I went downhill. I stayed at 15 mph for awhile and then coasted until I stopped.
5. The altitude of the space shuttle increased steadily until we couldn't see it any more.
6. We were driving at a constant speed of 50 mph on the highway when the transmission went out. Then we coasted to a stop.

Activity 3

1. After school, half the students in our class are in the band, $\frac{1}{4}$ play soccer, and another $\frac{1}{4}$ work.

2. I spent more of my homework time doing math than any other subject. I study English or reading $\frac{1}{4}$ of the time. I spend the same amount of time (about $\frac{1}{8}$) on science, spelling, and social studies.

3. In town, $\frac{2}{3}$ of the residents live in single-family homes, $\frac{1}{6}$ live in two-family homes, and $\frac{1}{6}$ live in apartments.

4. Nearly $\frac{3}{4}$ of the people who attended Oktoberfest rode the roller coaster, about $\frac{1}{8}$ rode the Ferris wheel, and the same number (about $\frac{1}{16}$) rode the other rides. Almost no one rode the upside-down rocket.

5. There are 8 hours in a typical work day.

6. Of the students in our class, $\frac{1}{20}$ can ride a unicycle.

Extending the Activities

- Have students write longer stories to go with one of the graphs.

- Challenge students to draw their own graphs and make up stories to go with them.

- Ask students to collect examples of graphs from newspapers and magazines and write about them.

Every Graph Tells a Story

What story might each of these graphs be telling?

1.
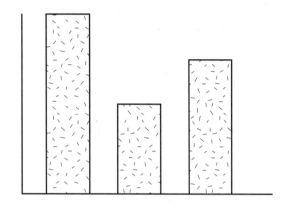

2.
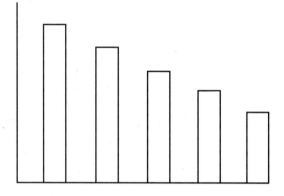

3.
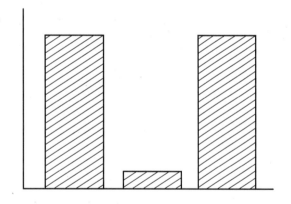

4.
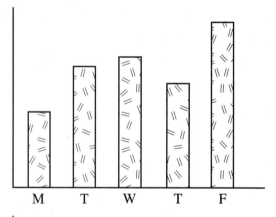

5.
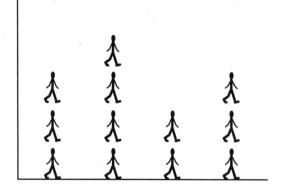

6.
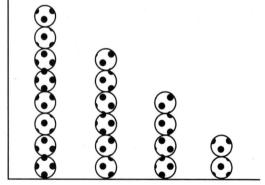

Every Graph Tells a Story

What story might each of these graphs be telling?

1.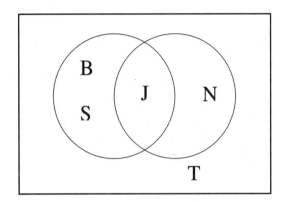

2.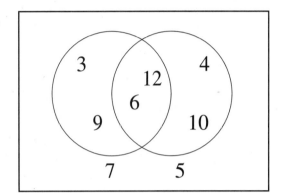

3.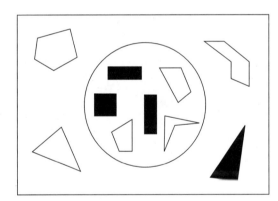

4.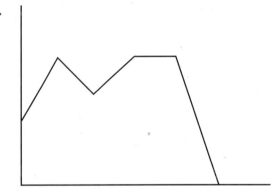

5.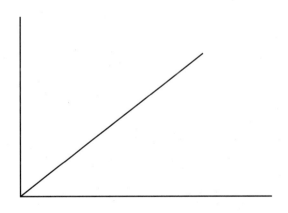

6.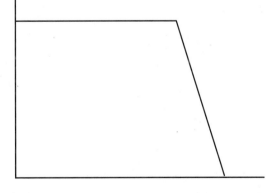

Every Graph Tells a Story

What story might each of these graphs be telling?

1.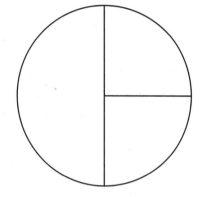

2.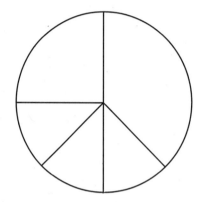

3.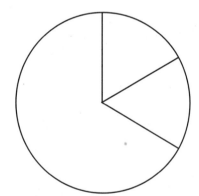

4.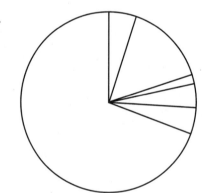

5.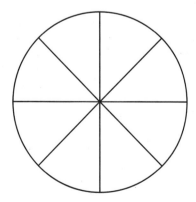

6.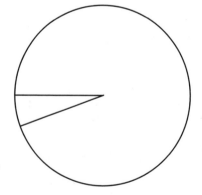

Letter Fractions

Number Sense Focus

• Multiple representation

Number Focus

• Activities 1–3: Fractions, percents

Mathematical Background

For many students, fractions are abstract concepts, related only to symbols. It is important that students experience fractions as representing a variety of concrete situations. Modeling fractions with letters and words is particularly powerful in clarifying the similarities and differences between equivalent fractions. For example, while the letter *t* occurs a different number of times in the words *at, tact,* and *totter,* it forms half of each of them.

Using the Activities

In these activities, students form connections between the number of letters in a word and the number of times a particular letter occurs in that word.

1. In Activity 1, check that students understand the task. You may wish to go through the first question with the class or ask some preliminary questions:

   • (Point to a word in the box.) How many letters are in this word?

   • How many times does the letter *a* (or *b* or *c*) appear in this word?

   • What fraction of the letters in this word are the letter *a*?

   • If *a* forms half of the letters in a word, what does that tell you about the number of letters in the word?

2. Have students work individually or in pairs to answer the questions. Remind them that each answer is one of the words in the box.

3. Go through the answers with the class, and discuss their strategies. For example, a student might report, "If $\frac{2}{3}$ of the letters are the same, the word must have 3 or 6 or 9 letters. I went through each word until I found one that worked." Leave time for some students who have made up their own examples to present them.

4. Use Activities 2 and 3 in the same way.

Solutions

Activity 1

1. a. all
    b. alphabet
    c. consonants
    d. the, letter
    e. of, so
    f. so, of, consonants

Activity 2

1. sadness: $\frac{1}{7}$; happiness: $\frac{1}{9}$

Activity 3

1. $\frac{1}{2}$
2. a. Texas
    b. Indiana
    c. Illinois
    d. Missouri
    e. Kansas
    f. Alabama
    g. California

Extending the Activities

• •

• Challenge students to make up their own set of letter fraction challenges.

• Have students carry out a word search to see how many words they can discover in which one letter forms $\frac{1}{3}$ *or more* or $\frac{1}{2}$ *or more* of the word.

• Ask students to choose a letter and find words for which that letter is $\frac{1}{2}, \frac{1}{3}, \frac{1}{4}, \frac{1}{5}, \ldots$ of the word.

Letter Fractions

The letter *a* is a vowel. So are the letters *e, i, o,* and *u*.

All the other letters of the alphabet are consonants.

---

1. Which word in the box above does each statement describe?

   a. $\frac{2}{3}$ of its letters are the same.

   b. $\frac{1}{4}$ of its letters are the same.

   c. 30% of its letters are the same.

   d. $\frac{1}{3}$ of its letters are *t*.

   e. 50% of its letters are *o*.

   f. 50% of its letters are *o* or *n*.

2. Make up another question like these, and write the question with its answer.

Letter Fractions

1. What fraction of each of these words consists of the letter *a*?

   ## Sadness   Happiness

2. Write a word in which the letter *a* forms

   a. $\frac{1}{2}$ of the word.

   b. $\frac{1}{3}$ of the word.

   c. $\frac{1}{4}$ of the word.

   d. $\frac{1}{5}$ of the word.

   e. $\frac{1}{6}$ of the word.

   f. 100% of the word.

   g. 40% of the word.

3. Make up another question like these, and write the question with its answer.

Letter Fractions

1. The letter *o* is $\frac{1}{7}$ of the letters in the word Vermont. What fraction of the word Ohio consists of the letter *o*?

2. Identify each of these state names.

    a. *x* is $\frac{1}{5}$

    b. *a* is $\frac{2}{7}$, i is $\frac{2}{7}$, and *n* is $\frac{2}{7}$

    c. *i* is $\frac{3}{8}$ and *l* is $\frac{1}{4}$

    d. *i* is $\frac{1}{4}$, *s* is $\frac{1}{4}$, and *m* is $\frac{1}{8}$

    e. *a* is $\frac{1}{3}$, *s* is $\frac{1}{3}$, and *k* is $\frac{1}{6}$

    f. *a* is $\frac{4}{7}$ and *b* is $\frac{1}{7}$

    g. *a* is 20%, *i* is 20%, *f* is 10%, and *c* is 10%

3. Make up another question like these, and write the question with its answer.

EXPERIENCE 30

Tile Patterns

Number Sense Focus

- Multiple representation

Number Focus

- Activities 1–3: Fractions

Mathematical Background

• •

An understanding of fractions goes beyond the mechanical counting of *x* units out of *y*. Work with physical models can help students develop their innate sense of the meaning of fractions.

Using the Activities

• •

In these activities, students are shown a tile design and asked what fraction of the pattern consists of each type of tile. Students cannot see—and therefore cannot count—all the tiles of each type. Instead, they must analyze the pattern and impose their own structure on it. If possible, students should work on their analysis in their heads without the use of pencil and paper.

1. In Activity 1, ask two or three students to describe the pattern. It is likely that they will analyze the pattern in quite different ways, even though they agree on the solution. Put the emphasis on clear descriptions and reasoning. Ask how many different types of tiles there are, which type is the most frequent in the pattern, and which type is the least frequent.

2. Ask students to discuss individually or in pairs what fraction of the pattern is composed of each type of tile. If students are struggling with the fractional ideas, ask how many of each tile they would need if the floor required, say, 80 tiles in all.

3. Ask some students to report their conclusions to the class. Encourage them to describe the strategies they used. These are some strategies students have offered:

   - "Half the tiles are white, because they are arranged like the white squares of a chess board. That leaves half to share between black and gray, so about $\frac{1}{4}$ of the tiles are gray and $\frac{1}{4}$ are black."

- "The whole pattern is made up of little 2-by-2 squares of tiles, all the same. Each 2-by-2 square has two white tiles, one gray tile, and one black tile, so the whole pattern must have $\frac{1}{2}$ white, $\frac{1}{4}$ black, and $\frac{1}{4}$ gray tiles."

- "Each row is made half of white tiles, and the rest are $\frac{1}{2}$ black and $\frac{1}{2}$ gray. So, $\frac{1}{2}$ of the tiles are white, and since $\frac{1}{2}$ of a $\frac{1}{2}$ is a $\frac{1}{4}$, $\frac{1}{4}$ are gray and $\frac{1}{4}$ are black."

4. Use Activities 2 and 3 in the same way.

Solutions

Activity 1

$\frac{1}{2}$ white tiles, $\frac{1}{4}$ black tiles, $\frac{1}{4}$ gray tiles (the smallest repeating unit is a 2-by-2 square)

Activity 2

$\frac{12}{25}$ dark gray tiles, $\frac{1}{25}$ pattern tiles, $\frac{4}{25}$ light gray tiles, $\frac{8}{25}$ white tiles (the smallest repeating unit is a 5-by-5 square)

Activity 3

$\frac{1}{2}$ white tiles, $\frac{1}{4}$ flower-design tiles, $\frac{1}{8}$ gray tiles, $\frac{1}{8}$ black tiles (the smallest repeating unit is a 2-by-4 rectangle)

Extending the Activities

- Let students create their own tile patterns on grid paper for other students to analyze. A clear repeating pattern must be used, containing no more than three or four types of tiles.

Tile Patterns

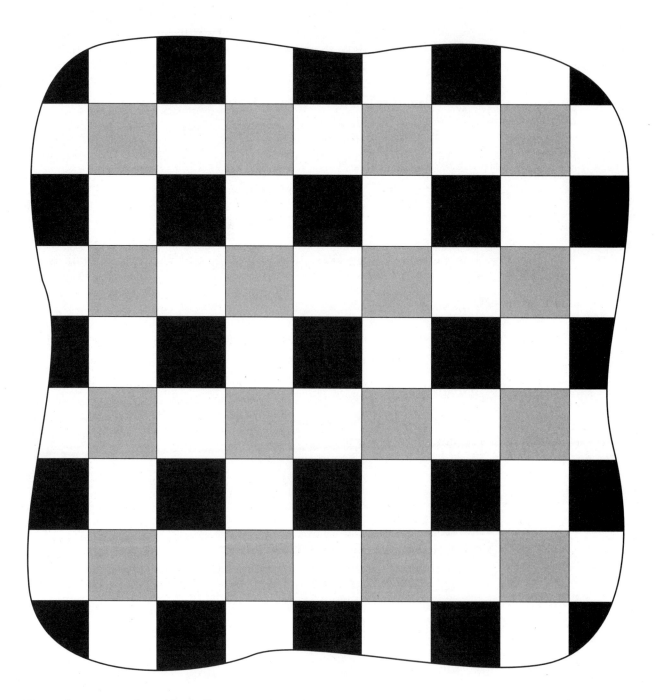

Here is part of a tiled floor. What fraction of the *whole* pattern is each type of tile?

Number SENSE / Grades 4–6

Tile Patterns

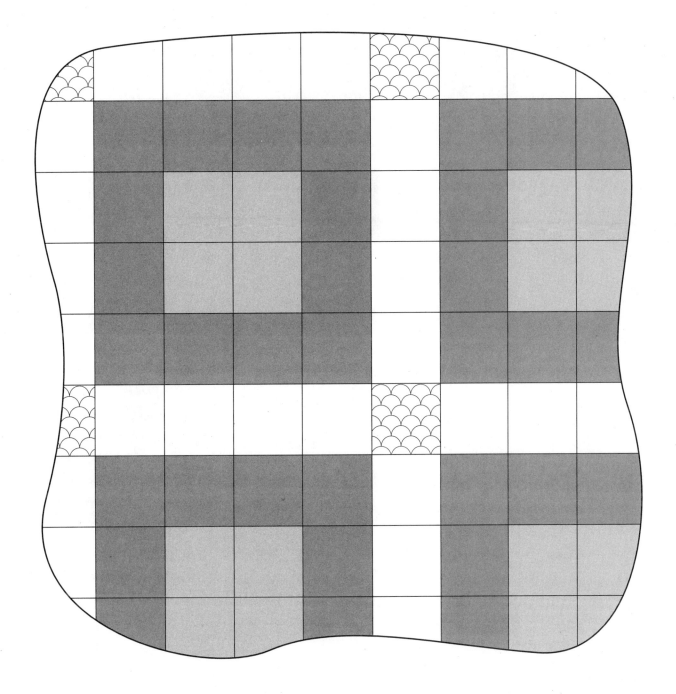

Here is part of a tiled floor. What fraction of the *whole* pattern is each type of tile?

Tile Patterns

Here is part of a tiled floor. What fraction of the *whole* pattern is each type of tile?

· ·

Finding Equivalent Products

Number Sense Focus

- Multiple representation
- Mental computation

Number Focus

- Activities 1–2: Whole numbers, fractions

Mathematical Background
· · · · · · · · · · · · · · · · · · · ·

Working with equivalent products helps students think about numbers more flexibly. For example, recognizing that five 10¢ coins, two 25¢ coins, one 50¢ coin, and four 10¢ coins plus two 5¢ coins are all ways to represent 50¢ requires an understanding of factors and of relationships among numbers.

Using the Activities
· · · · · · · · · · · · · · · · · · · ·

These activities provide opportunities for finding and using equivalent products. They will stimulate discussion and are particularly effective for small-group work that is later shared with the class.

1. Show the top half of Activity 1. As a class, make a list of the factors from the box that will make the Target Number of 24.

2. Stimulate discussion with questions such as these:
    - Which two factors have a product of 24? (12×2, 8×3, 24×1; 6×4)
    - Which three factors have a product of 24? ($2 \times 3 \times 4$, $2 \times 2 \times 6$; If some students want to include 1 and say that $12 \times 2 \times 1$ is different from 12×2, this is an opportunity to discuss the Fundamental Theorem of Arithmetic.)
    - Which four factors have a product of 24? ($2 \times 2 \times 2 \times 3$)
    - Did anyone use 0? (No, because any product involving 0 as a factor will be 0.)

3. Show the bottom half of Activity 1. Ask how the numbers in this box are different from the numbers in the upper box. (The 0 has been replaced with a 5.) Ask for a couple of solutions to make sure everyone is on the right track before students or groups make their own lists of solutions.

4. In Activity 2, students are presented with new targets and numbers.

Solutions

Activity 1

1. Some possibilities: 2×12, 3×8, 4×6, $2 \times 3 \times 4$, $2 \times 2 \times 2 \times 3$, $2 \times 2 \times 6$

2. Some possibilities: $5 \times 2 \times 24$, $5 \times 6 \times 8$, $5 \times 4 \times 12$, $5 \times 2 \times 3 \times 8$, $5 \times 2 \times 2 \times 3 \times 4$

   a. Some possibilities: 40, 80, 240
   b. yes; $120 \times 2 = 240$
   c. yes; $\frac{1}{2} \times 480 = 240$

Activity 2

1. Some possibilities: 1×40, 2×20, 4×10, 5×8, $2 \times 2 \times 10$, $2 \times 4 \times 5$

2. Some possibilities: $2 \times 5 \times 40$, $5 \times 5 \times 8 \times 2$, 20×20, $4 \times 5 \times 20$

   a. Some possibilities: 50, 100, 200
   b. Some possibilities: $\frac{1}{2}$ and $\frac{1}{4}$; $\frac{1}{2} \times 2 \times 5 \times 20 \times 40$ and $\frac{1}{4} \times 4 \times 5 \times 20 \times 40$

Extending the Activities

• •

- Ask students for examples of how different representations of 24 (or 240) are used (for example, 24 hours in a day, 4 six packs of soda in a case, 240 hours in 10 days).

- Which of two boxes, one with a volume of 640 cubic feet the other with a volume of 1000 cubic feet, gives the box with the greatest number of possible whole-number dimensions? Explain your answer. (The factors of 640 are $2 \times 2 \times 2 \times 2 \times 2 \times 2 \times 2 \times 5$; the factors of 1000 are $2 \times 2 \times 2 \times 5 \times 5 \times 5$. Since 640 has more factors, a box of this volume has more possible whole number dimensions.)

- Ask students for the dimensions of boxes that have the same number of units of volume as they do units of surface area (a 6-by-6-by-6 box is one possibility, as its volume is $6 \times 6 \times 6 = 216$ cubic units and its surface area is $6 \times 36 = 216$ square units).

- Have students work in groups. One student chooses the dimensions of a box and tells the other group members the volume and a clue or two, such as the area of one face or the fact that no two dimensions are the same. Others in the group try to find the box's dimensions. This illustrates the idea that containers with different dimensions can have the same volume–a real-world application of equivalent products.

Finding Equivalent Products

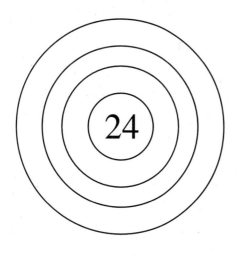

1. Using any values from the box, list as many products equal to the Target Number as you can. Values may be used more than once.

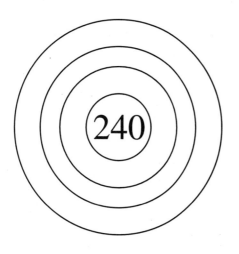

2. Using any values from the box, list as many products equal to the Target Number as you can. Values may be used more than once.

   a. What other useful numbers could be added to the box?

   b. Would 120 be useful in the box? Explain.

   c. Would $\frac{1}{2}$ and 480 be useful in the box? Explain.

Finding Equivalent Products

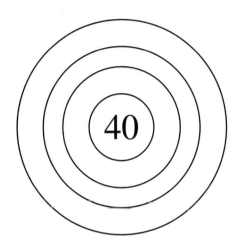

1	2	4	5
8	10	20	40

1. Using any values from the box, list as many products equal to the Target Number as you can. Values may be used more than once.

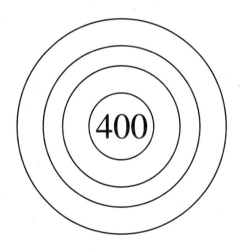

1	2	4	5
8	20	40	

2. Using any values from the box, list as many products equal to the Target Number as you can. Values may be used more than once.

    a. What other useful numbers could be added to the box?

    b. Name two fractions that could go in the box to make the Target Number. Explain why they would be useful.

EXPERIENCE 32

• •

Finding Equivalent Sums

Number Sense Focus

- Multiple representation
- Mental computation

Number Focus

- Activities 1–3: Whole numbers

Mathematical Background

• •

The abilities to recognize compatible numbers and equivalent sums are valuable number sense skills. For example, $0.65 + $0.35 and $0.71 + $0.29 are each equivalent to $1.00. Familiarity with compatible numbers promotes mental computation and estimation, and it encourages students to take advantage of patterns they observe.

Using the Activities

• •

These activities provide opportunities for finding and using equivalent sums. They will stimulate discussion and are particularly effective for small-group work that is later shared with the class. You may want to distribute a paper copy of the boxes of numbers to individuals or small groups.

1. Explore Activity 1 as a class. Questions such as these will help stimulate discussion:

    - If one addend is less than 50, what can you say about the other addend? (It must be more than 50.)

    - If one addend is odd, what do you know about the other addend? (It is also odd.)

    - If one addend ends in 5, what can be said about the other addend? (It also ends in 5.)

2. Give students time to work on Activity 2. Encourage students to share relationships between pairs of numbers that total 1000.

3. Activity 3 describes a picture frame with a specific perimeter and asks students to find the possible dimensions of the frame. This illustrates how areas of different dimensions can have the same perimeter and allows students to explore the relationship between area and perimeter.

Solutions

Activity 1

1. 11
2. Answers will vary.
3. 50 (from 1 + 99 to 50 + 50) or 51 (if you count 0 + 100)

Activity 2

1. a. 500, 333
    b. Answers will vary.
    c. 500 or 501 (if you count 0 + 1000)

Activity 3

1. Any number pair (whole numbers, fractions, and decimals) that totals 50 is a solution.
2. A square 25 cm on each side will produce the greatest area.

Extending the Activities

- Ask students when it would be useful to be able to find a number pair that totals $20.

- Call out a money amount (say, $5). Ask someone else to call out how much of that amount was spent (say, $4.85). Ask: How much change was given? As students become familiar with this game, have them call out both the money amount and the amount spent.

- Have students work in groups. One student chooses the dimensions of a rectangular frame and tells the others the perimeter of the frame and maybe another clue, such as the length of one side or the difference between the lengths of adjacent sides. Others in the group try to find the dimensions of the frame.

Finding Equivalent Sums

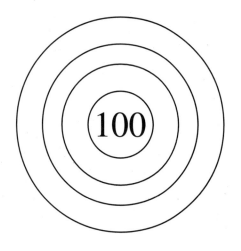

10	25	33	47	55
2	76	67	88	12
90	53	75	5	24
40	95	45	98	60
15	77	11	85	23

Using any values from the box, list as many pairs of numbers that add to the Target Number as you can.

1. Which number(s) in the box did not have a "partner" to total 100?

2. List some additional pairs of whole numbers that will total 100.

3. How many pairs of whole numbers will total 100? Explain how you found your answer.

Finding Equivalent Sums

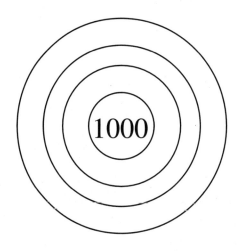

125	200	400	750	300
500	875	333	700	600
205	250	445	888	112
800	65	795	935	555

1. Using any values from the box, list as many pairs of numbers that add to the Target Number as you can.

    a. Which number(s) in the box do not have a "partner" to total 1000?

    b. List some additional pairs of whole numbers that will total 1000.

    c. How many pairs of whole numbers will total 1000? Explain how you found your answer.

Finding Equivalent Sums

Suppose you have a strip of wood that is 100 centimeters long, and you want to make a rectangular picture frame using all of your wood.

1. What are several different dimensions that are possible for your frame?

2. What frame would you make if you wanted to enclose the greatest area? Explain how you decided.

• •

Exploring Number Relationships

$$\frac{1}{2} \quad 50$$

$49\frac{1}{2} + \frac{1}{2} = 50$

$\frac{1}{2}$ is 50%

$\frac{1}{2}$ of 100 is 50

$25 \div 50 = \frac{1}{2}$

$$2 \quad 5$$

5 is 3 is more than 2

2 is 3 less than 5

2 is $\frac{2}{5}$ of 5

$2\frac{1}{2} \times 2 = 5$

$$3 \quad 4 \quad 5$$

three consecutive numbers

the middle number is 4

the sides of a right triangle

three numbers whose mean is 4

Every number is related to other numbers in many ways. The recognition of multiple relationships among numbers is one of the hallmarks of people with good number sense.

Recognizing relationships between numbers often makes a calculation simpler. For example, we can reason about 19×8 in many ways:

- $8 = 2 \times 2 \times 2$, so $19 \times 8 = 19 \times 2 \times 2 \times 2$, which is the same as double 19 to get 38, then double 38 to get 76, then double 76 to get 152.

- $19 = 20 - 1$, so $19 \times 8 = 20 \times 8 - 1 \times 8 = 160 - 8 = 152$.

- $19 = 10 + 9$, so $19 \times 8 = 10 \times 8 + 9 \times 8 = 80 + 72 = 152$.

The greater the number of relationships among numbers that are recognized, the more choices that are available.

In mental computation, the numbers 10 and 100 are particularly useful, as are compatible numbers. Number relationships are also used in estimation. For example, noticing the relationship between each fraction and $\frac{1}{2}$ makes it possible to estimate $\frac{3}{7} + \frac{4}{9}$ as less than 1 easily and confidently. Relationships also exist among sequences of numbers. For example, 1, 1, 2, 3, 5, 8, 13, . . . and 3, 6, 12, 24, 48, . . . are two forms of growth that demonstrate regular relationships between successive numbers in a sequence.

Recognizing such patterns helps us to identify trends and regularities in data and to notice when a number seems to be out of place because it does not fit the pattern.

These activities encourage students to explore number relationships and to take advantage of the relationships they observe.

Find a Connection

Number Sense Focus

- Number relationships
- Mental computation

Number Focus

- Activities 1–3: Whole numbers

Mathematical Background

When we compute mentally, we constantly discover and create relationships between numbers. For example, when mentally computing 4 kg of fertilizer at $3.95 a kg, we may relate this to $4 \times \$4 - 4 \times 5¢$. When adding 87 and 35, we may think of 87 as $100 - 13$, and 35 as $13 + 22$ to get an answer of $100 + 22 = 122$.

Using the Activities

These activities encourage students to make both simple and more complex connections among sets of three numbers.

1. The numbers in Activity 1 lend themselves to simple addition, subtraction, and multiplication relationships, such as $4 \times 8 = 32$, $11 + 21 = 32$, and $35 - 32 = 3$. Show the group of numbers, and invite students to choose three numbers to connect. Give them an example, such as $5 + 4 = 9$.

2. Invite individuals to name the three numbers and state the relationship. If students have not used less obvious types of relationships—such as the fact that 4, 8, and 32 share a factor of 4—offer an example, and challenge them to think of another. Make a class list of these relationships, and add additional relationships as students think of them.

3. Use Activities 2 and 3 in the same way. The choices in Activity 2 lend themselves to extended basic-fact relationships, such as $4 \times 30 = 120$

and $40 \times 30 = 1200$. The numbers in Activity 3 lend themselves to addition and subtraction relationships between two- and three-digit numbers, such as $48 + 71 = 119$ and $94 - 23 = 71$.

Solutions

Activity 1

Possible answers: $5 \times 7 = 35$; $15 - 12 = 3$; $21 \div 7 = 3$; 3, 4, and 5 are consecutive numbers; 7, 8, and 9 have a mean of 8.

Activity 2

Possible answers: $1200 \div 600 = 2$; 30 is half of 60 and 60 is half of 120; 8, 80, and 160 all have 8 as a factor; 20, 30, and 40 are multiples of 10.

Activity 3

Possible answers: $62 - 48 = 14$; $14 + 85 = 99$; 23, 37, and 131 are prime numbers; 60, 62, and 94 are even numbers; 60, 74, and 99 are all possible scores on a 100-point test.

Extending the Activities

• Give students 2 or 3 minutes to write as many connections as they can for sets of three numbers in a given set of numbers.

• Challenge students to create a set of 10 numbers with as many interesting relationships as possible.

• Give students a Start and a Finish Number, and challenge them to produce as many different ways as they can to get from one to the other. For example, starting at 6 and ending at 24 can be accomplished in these ways: $6 + 18 = 24$, $6 \times 4 = 24$, $6 \times 10 - 36 = 24$, $6 + 10 + 10 - 2 = 24$.

Find a Connection

Choose any three numbers, and show how they are related.

35   **7**   **21**

9

4

15   **8**

12

32

3

5   **11**

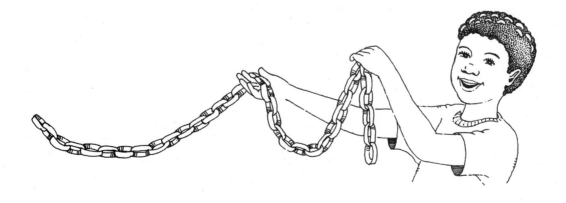

Find a Connection

Choose any three numbers, and show how they are related.

30   600   20
              90

120   4   160

                        8
              80
40
      1200
                   3

2   800
                        60

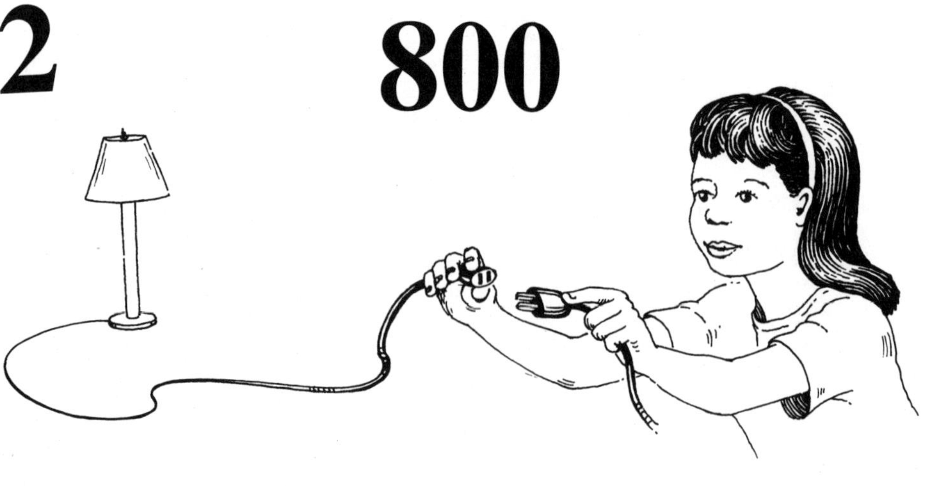

Find a Connection

Choose any three numbers, and show how they are related.

14   37   74

94   71   99

                85   51

48   119   23

62   131   60

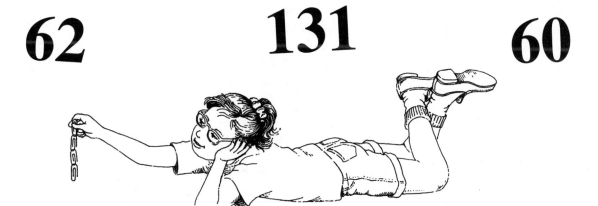

EXPERIENCE 34

•••••••••••••••••••••••••

Continue the Sequence

Number Sense Focus

• Number relationships

Number Focus

• Whole numbers

Mathematical Background

•••••••••••••••••••••••••

The ability to notice patterns—and to create them—is an integral part of good number sense.

Using the Activities

•••••••••••••••••••••••••

In these activities, students are shown a sequence of two or three numbers and are asked to continue the sequence according to some logical rule. The emphasis is not on spotting the pattern (as there is always more than one possibility) but on using one's imagination to create a pattern that works.

1. Show the first sequence in Activity 1, and invite the students to suggest ways the pattern might continue. Emphasize that there is more than one correct answer and that any pattern is correct if there is a logical explanation for it. Record all reasonable suggestions on the board to emphasize the variety possible, without singling out more complex suggestions as being better. Continue with the other sequences.

2. Use Activities 2 and 3 in the same way. It is unlikely that students will produce more than one pattern for the examples in Activity 3.

Solutions

Activity 1
Listed below are possible solutions for the sequences.

1. 1, 2, 3, 4, . . . (+ 1) or 1, 2, 4, 8, . . . (× 2)
2. 1, 3, 5, 7, . . . (odd numbers) or 1, 3, 1, 3, . . . (+ 2 then − 2)
3. 1, 4, 7, 10, . . . (+ 3) or 1, 4, 16, 64, . . . (× 4)

4. 1, 5, 9, 13, . . . (+ 4) or 1, 5, 25, 125, . . . (× 5)
5. 1, 1, 2, 2, 3, 3, . . . (+ 1 each two numbers) or 1, 1, 1, 1, . . . (constant repeating pattern)
6. 2, 4, 6, 8, . . . (even numbers) or 2, 4, 8, 16, . . . (× 2)
7. 4, 2, 0, –2, . . . (– 2) or 4, 2, 1, 1/2, . . . (× $\frac{1}{2}$)
8. 1, 10, 100, 10,000, . . . (× 10) or 1, 10, 19, 28, . . . (+ 9)

Activity 2

1. 1, 2, 3, 4, 5, . . . (+ 1) or 1, 2, 3, 5, 8, . . . (+ previous number)
2. 1, 2, 4, 8, 16, . . . (× 2) or 1, 2, 4, 7, 11, . . . (+ 1, + 2, + 3, . . .)
3. 1, 2, 5, 10, 17, . . . (+ consecutive odd numbers) or 1, 2, 5, 12, 29, . . . (double the number + the number before it)
4. 1, 2, 6, 16, 44, . . . (sum of the two previous numbers × 2) or 1, 2, 6, 42, 1806, . . . (the previous number × itself + itself)
5. 1, 3, 2, 4, 3, 5, 4, . . . (+ 2, – 1, + 2, – 1, . . .) or 1, 3, 2, 1, 3, 2, . . . (repeating sequence)
6. 1, 3, 5, 7, 9, . . . (odd numbers) or 1, 3, 5, 1, 3, 5, . . . (repeating sequence)
7. 4, 2, 0, –2, . . . (– 2)
8. 1, 4, 9, 16, 25, . . . (consecutive numbers squared)
   1, 4, 9, 16, 25, . . . (+ 3, + 5, + 7, + 9, . . .)

Activity 3

1. 6, 8, 10, 12, 14, 16, . . . (+ 2)
2. 7, 13, 19, 25, 31, 37, . . . (+ 6)
3. 100, 87, 74, 61, 48, 35, . . . (– 13)
4. 891, 792, 693, 594, 495, 396, . . . (– 99)
5. 2, 4, 8, 16, 32, 64, . . . (× 2)
6. 2, 6, 18, 54, 162, 486, . . . (× 3)
7. 2, 6, 12, 20, 30, 42, . . . (+ 4, + 6, + 8, . . .)
8. 2, 6, 20, 44, 78, 122, . . . (+ 4, + 14, + 24, . . .)

Extending the Activities

• •

- Give students two numbers in a sequence—for example 1, 2—and challenge them to write as many ways of continuing it, with explanations, as they can in 3 minutes.

- Give students sequences with gaps—for example 1, __, 4 to continue in different ways.

- Students can produce and describe their own number sequences.

Continue the Sequence

Suggest two ways each sequence of numbers might continue.
Explain each sequence you find.

1. 1, 2,

2. 1, 3,

3. 1, 4,

4. 1, 5,

5. 1, 1,

6. 2, 4,

7. 4, 2,

8. 1, 10,

Number SENSE / Grades 4–6

Continue the Sequence

Suggest one or two ways each sequence of numbers might continue.
Explain each sequence you find.

1. 1, 2, 3,

2. 1, 2, 4,

3. 1, 2, 5,

4. 1, 2, 6,

5. 1, 3, 2,

6. 1, 3, 5,

7. 4, 2, 0,

8. 1, 4, 9,

Continue the Sequence

Suggest one way each sequence of numbers might continue.
Explain each sequence you find.

1. 6, 8, 10,

2. 7, 13, 19,

3. 100, 87, 74,

4. 891, 792, 693,

5. 2, 4, 8,

6. 2, 6, 18,

7. 2, 6, 12,

8. 2, 6, 20,

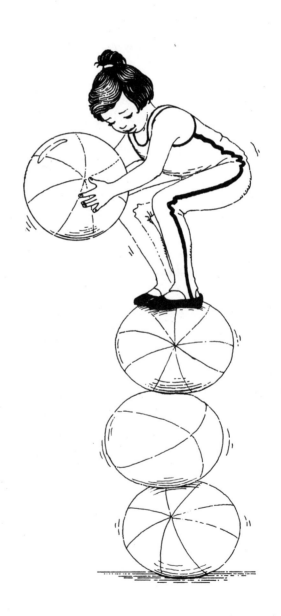

Name That Whole Number

Number Sense Focus

- Number relationships
- Multiple representation

Number Focus

- Activities 1–3: Whole numbers

Mathematical Background

Part of good number sense is recognizing different ways of expressing numbers and characteristics of those numbers. These activities give students a chance to name whole numbers that satisfy certain clues. They encourage thoughtful reflection about numbers.

Using the Activities

1. As a warm-up, ask students to describe different ways of representing $10, such as $5 + $5. Make a list of their ideas to demonstrate that many different answers exist. Extend their thinking by providing other clues for representations of $10, such as these:

   - The number of $1 bills is more than the number of $5 bills.

   - Only two bills are used.

   - Exactly six bills are used.

   - Nine bills and three coins are used.

2. Form teams of two to four students. Display the clues, or read each set of clues aloud. Ask each team to write one answer for each set of clues. Some clues are extraneous; teams should decide which clues are unnecessary for solving each mystery. Explain mathematical terms such as *square number* if necessary.

3. Follow a similar procedure for Activities 2 and 3.

Solutions

Activity 1

1. 500; Clues b and c *or* Clues b and d
2. 2; Clue c
3. 25; Clues a, c, and d
4. 47; Clues c and d

Activity 2

1. 500; Clues a, b, and d *or* Clues c and d
2. 360
3. 50; Clues a, c, and d *or* Clues b and c *or* Clues a, b, and d
4. 375; Clue d

Activity 3

1. 60
2. 1900; Clue a
3. 2,000,000; Clues a and b
4. 4900; Clues a and d *or* Clues a and e

Extending the Activities

• •

- Have teams create Mystery Number problems and exchange them with other teams.

- Ask each team to prepare a list of clues for a given number. Make a master list of all the clues, and discuss similarities and differences between the clues that teams developed.

Name That Whole Number

The Mystery Number	**Solution**

1. *Clue a:* is between 400 and 600

   Clue b: is greater than 450

   Clue c: is a multiple of 100

   Clue d: is a multiple of 500

   Mystery Number _____

   Unnecessary clues _____

2. *Clue a:* is a prime number

   Clue b: is an even number

   Clue c: is a one-digit number

   Mystery Number _____

   Unnecessary clues _____

3. *Clue a:* is a square number

   Clue b: is halfway between 20 and 30

   Clue c: is an odd number

   Clue d: is a two-digit number

   Mystery Number _____

   Unnecessary clues _____

4. *Clue a:* is within 3 numbers of 48

   Clue b: is a prime number

   Clue c: is a two-digit number

   Clue d: is not an even number

   Mystery Number _____

   Unnecessary clues _____

Name That Whole Number

The Mystery Number	**Solution**

1. *Clue a:* is a multiple of 500

    Clue b: is a three-digit number

    Clue c: is halfway between 0 and 1000

    Clue d: is an even number

    Mystery Number _____

    Unnecessary clues _____

2. *Clue a:* is a multiple of 30

    Clue b: is a multiple of 20

    Clue c: is between 350 and 400

    Mystery Number _____

    Unnecessary clues _____

3. *Clue a:* is a multiple of 50

    Clue b: has a square of 2500

    Clue c: has a cube of 125,000

    Clue d: is a two-digit number

    Mystery Number _____

    Unnecessary clues _____

4. *Clue a:* is more than 300

    Clue b: is less than 400

    Clue c: is a multiple of 75

    Clue d: is a multiple of 5

    Mystery Number _____

    Unnecessary clues _____

Name That Whole Number

The Mystery Number	**Solution**

1. *Clue a:* when divided by 10 is
   an even number

   Clue b: is a two-digit number

   Clue c: is divisible by 6

   Mystery Number _____

   Unnecessary clues _____

2. *Clue a:* is a four-digit number

   Clue b: when divided by 100 is
   an odd number

   Clue c: is more than 1700

   Clue d: is less than 2100

   Mystery Number _____

   Unnecessary clues _____

3. *Clue a:* is more than a 1000 thousands

   Clue b: is an even number

   Clue c: is the largest multiple of
   400,000 that is less than 2,150,000

   Mystery Number _____

   Unnecessary clues _____

4. *Clue a:* has one odd digit

   Clue b: is less than 5000

   Clue c: is more than 4800

   Clue d: is a perfect square

   Clue e: is divisible by 100

   Mystery Number _____

   Unnecessary clues _____

EXPERIENCE 36

Name a Decimal

Number Sense Focus

- Number relationships
- Multiple representation

Number Focus

- Activities 1–3: Decimals

Mathematical Background

Open-ended problems that involve certain operations and conditions stimulate flexible thinking. These activities provide opportunities for students to construct answers to satisfy certain clues, with a focus on decimals.

Using the Activities

1. As a warm-up, ask students to name a decimal larger than 0.5. Make a list of their suggestions to demonstrate the variety of possible answers.

2. Form teams of two to four students. Display the statement, or read it aloud. Ask each team to write one answer for each clue.

3. As a class, list several solutions for each statement. Have students explain how they decided upon their answers. You may need to remind students that whole numbers are also decimals; that is, 1 can be written as 1.0.

4. Follow a similar procedure for Activities 2 and 3.

Extending the Activities

- Have teams make up clues and exchange them with other teams.

- Find an example of a decimal used in a newspaper or magazine. Tell how the decimal was written (in symbols or in words). Tell why you think a decimal was used rather than a fraction or a percent.

Name a Decimal

Working in your team, make up one answer to fit each statement.

Possible Answers

1. A decimal between 3 and 4 _____

2. A decimal greater than 2.15 _____

3. A decimal less than 3 _____

4. Two decimals whose sum is 1 _____

5. Three decimals whose sum is
less than 0.8 _____

6. Two decimals whose difference
is between 0.1 and 0.2 _____

7. Five decimals whose sum is
between 2 and 3 _____

8. Three decimals whose sum is 1.25 _____

9. Two decimals with a difference
of 0.35 _____

10. Four decimals whose sum is 2.35 _____

Name a Decimal

Working in your team, make up one answer to fit each statement.

Possible Answers

1. A decimal between 0.3 and 0.4 _____

2. A decimal greater than 2.15 and less than 2.25 _____

3. A decimal less than 0.3 _____

4. Two decimals whose sum is 1.0 _____

5. Two decimals whose product is less than 1 _____

6. Two decimals whose product is is between 1 and 2 _____

7. Two decimals whose sum is between 0.4 and 0.6 _____

8. Three decimals whose product is between 10 and 15 _____

9. Two decimals whose quotient is less than 1 _____

10. Two decimals whose quotient is between 2 and 3 _____

Name a Decimal

Working in your team, make up one answer to fit each statement.

Possible Answers

1. Three decimals between 0.3 and 0.4 _____

2. A decimal greater than 2.15 and less than 2.16 _____

3. A decimal less than 0.03 _____

4. Two decimals whose difference is 0.98 _____

5. Three decimals whose product is less than 1 _____

6. Two decimals whose quotient is between 1 and 2 _____

7. Two decimals whose product is between 0.5 and 0.6 _____

8. Three decimals whose product is between 1.0 and 1.5 _____

9. Two decimals whose quotient is between 0.5 and 0.6 _____

10. Three decimals whose product is 6 _____

EXPERIENCE 37

•••••••••••••••••••••••••

Name a Fraction

Number Sense Focus

- Number relationships
- Multiple representation

Number Focus

- Activities 1–3: Fractions

Mathematical Background

•••••••••••••••••••••••••••••

As in Lesson 36, these open-ended activities ask students to construct answers that satisfy certain conditions, this time with a focus on fractions.

Using the Activities

•••••••••••••••••••••••••••••

1. As a warm-up, ask students to name a fraction between $\frac{1}{2}$ and 1. Whatever fraction is named, ask them for a fraction between that number and 1. Record their suggestions to show the wealth of possible answers. Encourage discussion of any patterns students discover.

2. Form teams of two to four students. Display the statement, or read it aloud. Ask each team to write one answer for each clue. You may need to remind students that whole numbers are also fractions; that is, the number 3 can be written as $\frac{6}{2}$, $\frac{9}{3}$, or $\frac{3}{1}$.

3. As a class, list several solutions for each clue. Ask students to explain how they decided on their answers. Follow a similar procedure for Activities 2 and 3.

Extending the Activities

•••••••••••••••••••••••••••••

- Have teams make up clues and exchange them with other teams.

- Have students find an example of a fraction used in a newspaper or magazine, explain how the fraction was written (in symbols or in words), and hypothesize about why a fraction was used rather than a decimal or a percent.

Name a Fraction

Working in your team, make up one answer to fit each statement.

Possible Answers

1. A fraction between $\frac{1}{4}$ and $\frac{1}{2}$ _____

2. A fraction greater than $\frac{3}{4}$ _____

3. A fraction less than $\frac{1}{3}$ _____

4. A fraction that is a little more than 1 _____

5. A fraction between 2 and 3 _____

6. A fraction near 0 _____

7. A fraction that is almost 1 _____

8. A fraction that is almost $\frac{1}{2}$ _____

9. A fraction between $\frac{1}{3}$ and $\frac{1}{4}$ _____

10. A fraction that is nearly 3 _____

Name a Fraction

Working in your team, make up one answer to fit each statement.

Possible Answers

1. Two fractions whose sum is 1 _____

2. Two fractions whose sum is almost 1 _____

3. Two fractions whose sum is near 0 _____

4. Two fractions whose sum is less than $\frac{1}{4}$ _____

5. Two fractions whose sum is more than 1 _____

6. Two fractions whose difference is almost 0 _____

7. Two fractions whose difference is about, but not exactly, $\frac{1}{2}$ _____

8. Three fractions whose sum is between 1 and 2 _____

9. Two fractions with a difference of exactly 1 _____

10. Two fractions, one of which is twice the other _____

Name a Fraction

Working in your team, make up one answer to fit each statement.

Possible Answers

1. Two fractions, one of which is four times the other

    _____

2. Two fractions whose quotient is 1

    _____

3. Two fractions whose quotient is $\frac{1}{2}$

    _____

4. Two fractions whose product is less than 1

    _____

5. Three fractions whose product is 0

    _____

6. Two fractions whose product is 1

    _____

7. Two fractions whose quotient is 0

    _____

8. Two fractions whose product is between $\frac{1}{2}$ and 1

    _____

9. Six fractions whose product is less than 1

    _____

10. Two fractions whose product is greater than 1

    _____

EXPERIENCE 38

Target Multiplication

Number Sense Focus

- Number relationships
- Estimation
- Mental computation

Number Focus

- Activities 1–2: Whole numbers

Mathematical Background

Exploring number relationships is an important part of determining the relative size of products. For example, recognizing that 10×285 is 2850 helps one conclude that 9×285 is less than 2850 without finding the exact product. Mental computation and estimation—and the use of lead digits and benchmarks—are also useful for finding upper and lower limits for results.

Using the Activities

1. Show the top third of Activity 1, and ask students to choose one factor from each box to make a product in the target range. Encourage them to explain their thinking. For example, students have offered these explanations:

    - "I know 10×28 is 280 and that is too small, so I think it is 11×28."
    - "I know 10×28 is 280, so 28 more would be over 300."
    - "I didn't even try the factors of 53 and 65 from Box 2 because I knew they were too big."

2. Ask students to choose one factor from each box to produce the largest possible product and one factor from each box to produce the smallest possible product. Students should generalize that the two largest factors will always produce the largest product and that the two smallest factors will always produce the smallest product.

3. Continue with the second and third sets of boxes.

4. Conduct Activities 2 in a similar way.

Solutions

Activity 1

1. 11 and 28
2. 22 and 81
3. 61 and 21, 71 and 21

Activity 2

1. 112 and 28
2. 19 and 815, 384 and 51
3. 62 and 2189

Extending the Activities

• •

• Decide on a target range. Have students construct numbers in two different boxes that would be appropriate and inappropriate for the predetermined range.

Target Multiplication

In each set, choose one factor from each box to make a product in the target range.

1.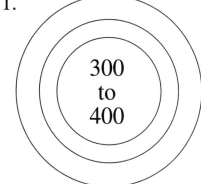

300
to
400

Box A	Box B
11	28
10	53
9	65

2.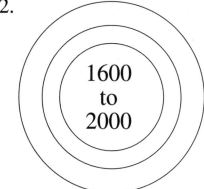

1600
to
2000

Box C	Box D
17	81
22	62
15	59

3.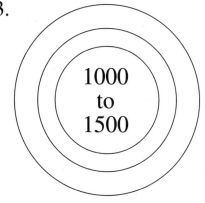

1000
to
1500

Box E	Box F
81	31
91	21
71	41
61	

Target Multiplication

In each set, choose one factor from each box to make a product in the target range.

1.

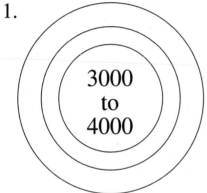

Box A	Box B
112	28
205	57
97	45

2.

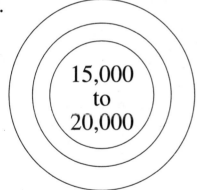

Box C	Box D
19	815
200	69
384	51

3.

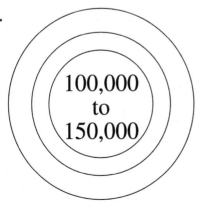

Box E	Box F
864	314
912	212
62	2189
200	

EXPERIENCE 39

• •

What Did I Buy?

Number Sense Focus

- Number relationships
- Mental computation

Number Focus

- Activities 1–3: Decimals

Mathematical Background

• •

Mental computation is greatly enhanced by the ability to recognize compatible numbers—for example, pairs of numbers that total a multiple of 10 or 100, such as 7 and 3, 22 and 28, 36 and 64. In this experience, students may use the bridging-100 strategy for adding numbers such as 88 and 34 by reasoning, for example, that 88 and 12 make 100, plus 22 is 122.

Using the Activities

• •

In these activities, students focus on finding compatible money amounts that total $5.00.

In Activities 1 and 3, all amounts are multiples of 25¢.

1. In Activity 1, invite students to find two items that together cost exactly $5 and to explain how they calculated the sum. For example: "The hot dog and the tostada make $5, because 75¢ + 25¢ = $1, and $1 + $1 + $3 = $5."

2. Use Activities 2 and 3 in the same way.

Solutions

Activity 1

Some possibilities: apple and spaghetti, medium juice and chicken, sandwich and green salad

Activity 2

Some possibilities: pen and stapler, note pad and appointment book, envelopes and binder

Activity 3

Some possibilities: small ball, golf balls, and dart board; whistle, tennis balls, and swimming goggles; safety glasses, jacks, and jump rope

Extending the Activities

- Ask students to find pairs of items that cost $3, $4, or $6.

- Name pairs of items at random, and challenge students to give their total cost.

- Challenge students to give the total cost of all the items in each activity.

- Invite students to list other sums of money that total $5.

What Did I Buy?

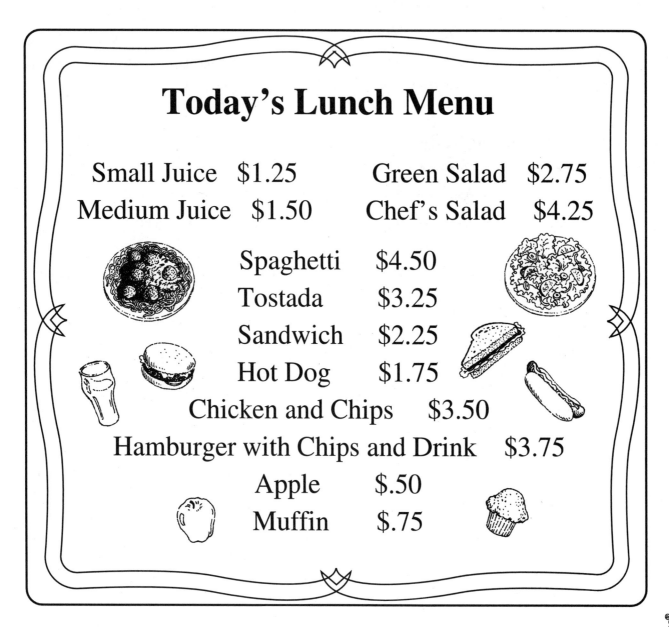

Today's Lunch Menu

Small Juice $1.25   Green Salad $2.75
Medium Juice $1.50   Chef's Salad $4.25

Spaghetti $4.50
Tostada $3.25
Sandwich $2.25
Hot Dog $1.75
Chicken and Chips $3.50
Hamburger with Chips and Drink $3.75
Apple $.50
Muffin $.75

Find pairs of items that cost exactly $5.

What Did I Buy?

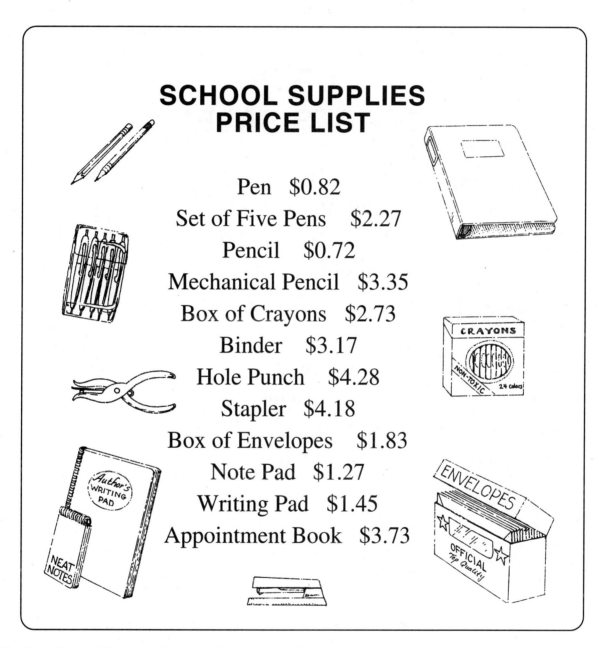

SCHOOL SUPPLIES PRICE LIST

Pen $0.82

Set of Five Pens $2.27

Pencil $0.72

Mechanical Pencil $3.35

Box of Crayons $2.73

Binder $3.17

Hole Punch $4.28

Stapler $4.18

Box of Envelopes $1.83

Note Pad $1.27

Writing Pad $1.45

Appointment Book $3.73

Find pairs of items that cost exactly $5.

What Did I Buy?

SUPER SPORTS SALE!

Small Ball $0.25
Golf Balls $1.75
Tennis Balls $2.00
Set of Jacks $1.00
Darts $2.50
Dart Board $3.00
Safety Glasses $2.75
Swimming Goggles $2.25
Jump Rope $1.25
Baseball Cap $1.50
Whistle $0.75

Find sets of three items that cost exactly $5.

Exploring Reasonableness

When an answer is **reasonable,**
we might say

- That's close.
- That's in the ballpark.
- It seems about right.
- Close enough.

When an answer is **unreasonable,**
we might say

- That's not even close.
- That's not even in the ballpark.
- That doesn't seem right.
- You have to be kidding.

Assessing whether computational results are reasonable is an important decision-making process that requires sensitivity to both the operations and the numbers involved. For example, consider these results:

A.	289	B.	289	C.	289	D.	289	E.	289	F.	289
	$\times\ 3$		$\times\ 3$		$\times\ 3$		$\times\ 3$		$\times\ 3$		$\times\ 3$
	1067		67		868		292		877		907

Recognizing that these results are incorrect requires reflection and analysis. The critical thinking required to assess such answers must be adjusted to fit the situation. The concept of reasonableness, for example, could be used to reject all but one of these results.

If you know the product of two odd numbers must be odd, you could reject the answer to C as being unreasonable, though it is very close to the correct answer. If you reason that $300 \times 3 = 900$, so 289×3 must be less than 900, you could reject the answers to A and F as being unreasonable. Though the answers to B and D are less than 900, they could be rejected because they are not as close to 900 as would be expected.

The answer to E is reasonable but incorrect. Checking for reasonableness only detects answers that are logically incorrect or clearly inappropriate.

The answer to E satisfies the tests for reasonableness that were applied above. Thus an answer may be incorrect and still be reasonable.

Reasonableness is difficult to define, but our goal is to encourage inquiry that will help students to think about the numbers, the operations, and the situation, and to make judgments. The more opportunities students have to think about results and the more they are challenged to decide what is reasonable, the more they will come to value the question, "Is this about what I expect?"

· ·

Making It Right

Number Sense Focus

- Reasonableness
- Relative size

Number Focus

- Activities 1, 2: Whole numbers
- Activity 3: Percents

Mathematical Background

· ·

When numbers are reported, it is important to think about their values and decide whether the information is reasonable. Personal experiences help students create personal benchmarks, which they can rely on when they evaluate whether something makes sense.

Using the Activities

· ·

In these activities, students read statements that report numerical values. Something is clearly wrong with each statement. To decide what correction is needed to make each statement reasonable, additional information may need to be collected from other students or resources.

1. As a warm-up, ask what is wrong with this statement: There are about 20,000 students in our school. Students should realize that the relative size of this number is too large. Encourage them to consider the consequences of having 20,000 students in the school. For example, if the school has 40 classrooms, it would mean having 500 students per classroom. If the cafeteria seats 200, it would take 100 lunch sessions for everyone to eat.

2. In each activity, reveal the statements one at a time. Ask students to identify what is wrong with each statement and to suggest how it might be corrected. Exploring the consequences of the original numerical values can promote thinking about their reasonableness.

Solutions

Activity 1

1. The typical allowance is clearly far less than $2000. (What would students do with a $2000 allowance?)
2. Anything in the range of 28° to 35° Celsius would be reasonable.
3. The distance is actually about 6000 km.
4. Australia is actually about 1/3 the size of North America.
5. The population of the United States is over 260,000,000.
6. The range is closer to 4000 to 5000 days.
7. The typical height is much less than 111 inches (which is over 9 feet).
8. Barring injuries and ejections, there are 11 players on a soccer team.
9. The number of days spent in most schools is closer to 180 to 200 days.
10. The actual time is closer to 6 hours a day.

Activity 2

1. The amount of cake is actually quadrupled.
2. Three German marks were worth about two United States dollars.
3. If you double the value of any two-digit number greater than 50, you will always get a three-digit number.
4. The average would actually be about
   $(30 + 30 + 30 + 30 + 30 + 30 + 40) \div 7$, or about 31° to 32°.
5. The temperature actually rose 55°.

Activity 3

1. Fat-free chips have no fat, meaning they have 100% less fat than regular potato chips.
2. 100% means it is certain to rain; no percentage larger than this makes sense.
3. The total increase is actually 125%. (This can be demonstrated by using an example. If I start with a $1 allowance and get a 50% increase, my new allowance is $1.50. A 50% increase on this would give me $2.25. The total increase, from $1 to $2.25, is 125%.)
4. Independent events cannot be added together. The chance of rain during the weekend is 0.75 (1 – chance of no rain, or $1 - \frac{1}{2} \times \frac{1}{2}$)
5. The average must be based on all the tests:
   $(80 + 80 + 80 + 100) \div 4 = 85\%$.

Extending the Activities

• •

- Ask students to construct statements with at least one incorrect bit of numerical information.

- Have students look for misleading advertising or other data in magazines and newspapers.

Making It Right

1. The average weekly allowance for a middle-school student is $2000.

2. It was very hot in our classroom today. The temperature was about 212° Celsius.

3. The distance from New York to Los Angeles is about 600 km.

4. Australia is about three times as large as North America.

5. The population of the United States is about 250,000.

6. A middle-school student has lived about 10,000 days.

7. The tallest student in our class is 111 inches tall.

8. Five soccer players from each team play during a soccer game.

9. We attend school about 360 days in a calendar year.

10. We spend about 6 minutes a day at school on a regular school day.

Making It Right

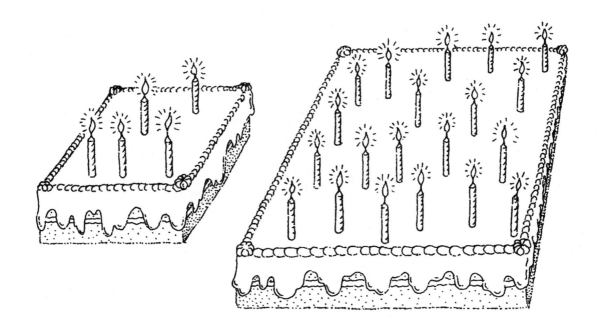

1. If you double the length and double the width of a rectangular cake, the amount of cake is doubled.

2. In September 1995, one German mark was worth about $0.65 of a United States dollar, so three U.S. dollars will buy about two German marks.

3. If you double the value of any two-digit number, you will get a three-digit number.

4. The average daily high temperature from Monday to Saturday was 30°. On Sunday, the daily high temperature was 40°. The average high temperature for the entire week was 35°.

5. Today's low temperature was ⁻25° and the high was 30°. The temperature rose 5°.

Making It Right

1. Super Spuds fat-free potato chips have 200% less fat than regular potato chips.

2. The chance of rain tomorrow is 200%.

3. A 50% increase in your allowance this month, followed by a 50% increase in your new allowance next month, is a total increase of 100%.

4. The chance of rain on Saturday is 50%. The chance of rain on Sunday is also 50%. Therefore, the chance of rain this weekend is 100%.

5. I scored 80% on my biology quiz three weeks in a row. This week I scored 100%. My average for the month is 90%.

Number SENSE / Grades 4–6

Reasonable Remainders

Number Sense Focus

- Reasonableness
- Mental computation

Number Focus

- Activity 1: Whole numbers, decimals

Mathematical Background

Division frequently results in quotients with remainders, which may be written as whole numbers, decimals, or fractions. Research shows that students often ignore the context in which division occurs and thus incorrectly interpret or simply misunderstand what the remainders represent. Calculator results offer many opportunities to interpret decimal remainders.

Using the Activity

These activities provide several contexts in which remainders are common and encourage students to think about what makes sense.

1. As a warm-up, ask the class to think about 13 students taking a trip in three cars. How many students could go in each car? Clearly the answer is not 4.3333333. Since people cannot be divided into thirds, it would make sense that four students ride in each of two cars and five students ride in the other car. If only four students can ride in a car, then another car is needed.

2. In the activity, ask students to solve each problem, using a calculator if necessary, and to explain what would be the best way to handle each remainder.

Solutions

1. 4 or 5
2. probably 65¢
3. probably 8 or 9 teams, depending on how many extra players are assigned to each team
4. 10 cases, although only 9 would be completely filled
5. 12 buses, only 11 of which would be full
6. 11 tiles plus $\frac{2}{3}$ of another, which means 12 tiles
7. probably 67¢
8. at least 11 tents
9. 8¢

Extending the Activity

· ·

- Ask students to construct a problem that has a quotient with a remainder and to explain how the remainder should be handled.

- Give students an answer, such as 17.25, and ask them to make up a division problem that would result in the answer.

Reasonable Remainders

13 ÷ 3
equals
4.3333. . .

1. If 13 students are going to a game in three cars, how many students will ride in each car?

2. A grocer sells two cans of soup for $1.29. How much would a customer pay for one can?

3. A total of 103 students want to play soccer. A soccer team has 11 players. How many teams can be formed?

4. How many cases are needed to pack 234 cans if each case holds 24 cans?

5. A total of 412 students will travel to Washington, D.C. on a school trip. Each bus will hold 36 students. How many buses will be needed?

6. The width of the ceiling in a room measures 140 inches. How many 1-square-foot ceiling tiles will be needed to make one row of tiles across the ceiling?

7. Grapefruit are priced at three for $2. How much would one grapefruit cost?

8. A camping trip involves 86 scouts. Each tent will sleep no more than 8 scouts. How many tents are needed?

9. Ten pieces of gum cost 71¢. If you wanted to sell the gum and not lose money, what is the lowest price per piece you could charge?

EXPERIENCE 42

What's Wrong with This Graph?

Number Sense Focus

- Reasonableness
- Relative size
- Estimation

Number Focus

- Activity 1: Percents

Mathematical Background

Circle graphs are particularly effective for showing 100% of something, a reason they frequently appear in magazines and newspapers. Most of the time the graphs are correct, but occasionally errors slip by the editors. Readers must always be alert for mistakes, and a sense of reasonableness is a powerful ally in detecting errors.

Using the Activity

1. Show the newspaper headline, which appeared in a local paper. Ask students to read and interpret the circle graph.

2. Encourage discussion and establish that reasonableness requires that the graph sections and written percents correspond. Ask: Are there some things you are sure are wrong? Are there some that are correct? Listen to their explanations to learn what benchmarks they are using.

3. Discuss the questions about the graph.

Solutions

Activity 1

1. Either the artist made errors in determining the areas or the reported percents were altered. Perhaps the labels should say that 45% of students buy a school lunch and 30% bring their own lunch. We don't know what is correct, but we do know some errors exist.

2. If 55% of students buy a school lunch, then over half of the circle should have been designated for this section. Also, 20% should be less than a quarter of the circle.

3. The benchmarks of $\frac{1}{2}$ (50%) and $\frac{1}{4}$ (25%) may be helpful.

4. Encourage different interpretations of the headline. However, just because the majority of students buy their lunch at school does not mean they like school lunches.

Extending the Activity

• Ask students to make a circle graph that correctly shows the percents reported.

• Have student take a survey of school lunches among students in the class and make a circle graph to summarize the results.

What's Wrong with This Graph?

SURPRISE!
Most Students Like School Lunches!

The headline above concluded that most students like school lunches. It reported results from a survey of students to support that conclusion. The data were given in a circle graph.

Students and School Lunches

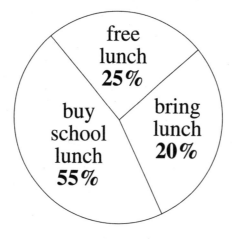

1. What errors can you find in this information?

2. How do you know this graph has errors?

3. What clues or benchmarks helped you detect the errors?

4. Do you think the headline reflects the survey results? Explain.

· ·

What's Wrong with This Picture?

Number Sense Focus

- Reasonableness
- Relative size
- Estimation

Number Focus

- Activity 1: Whole numbers

Mathematical Background

· ·

Benchmarks allow us to use what we know to determine whether values are reasonable. The more mathematics one learns and applies, the more benchmarks may be used to evaluate the reasonableness of a result.

Using the Activity

· ·

Commercial airplanes usually fly between 25,000 and 35,000 feet. Mt. McKinley in Alaska is 20,320 feet, meaning the highest mountain in the United States does not exceed 4 miles. These facts provide benchmarks that can raise a question about the reasonableness of the elevation reported in this activity.

1. Show the highway sign illustrated in the activity. Ask students what the terms *population* and *elevation* mean. Students might use an almanac or atlas to find the population and elevation of several cities in their state.

2. Encourage discussion to help identify the unit involved in determining population (people) and measuring elevation (feet or meters) and a range of reasonable values. Ask what units are probably implied on the sign. We often see population identified on road signs by a number without an identified unit. This elevation probably refers to feet, but in Mexico, Canada, Australia, and many other countries, elevation would be reported in meters.

3. Discuss the questions. Establish that reasonableness involves thoughtful interpretation of both the number and the unit.

Solutions

1. The population number may be right, but the elevation number is unreasonable.

2. No point on earth has an elevation of 50,000 feet. Very few planes even fly this high!

3. The numbers should probably be reversed. (Actually, this is exactly what is needed; the sign painter who made the real sign had exchanged the two numbers.)

4. Since 5280 feet are in a mile, an elevation of 6062 feet is just over a mile high. (Denver, which has an elevation of 5280 feet, is nicknamed the Mile-High city.)

5. Mt. Everest has an elevation of 29,028 feet.

6. The city is below sea level. The lowest point in New Orleans, for example, is 5 feet below sea level.

Extending the Activity

• •

- Ask students to find the elevation and population where they live, and to name a town or city with a higher elevation or a greater population. They might also research what city or country has the lowest elevation on earth.

What's Wrong with This Picture?

This sign was posted in a city in the western United States. It was several days before someone recognized some errors.

1. What is wrong with this sign?

2. How do you know that these numbers are incorrect?

3. How might this sign be corrected?

4. Why do you think this town was named One-Mile Flats?

5. What is the elevation of the highest mountain on earth?

6. Explain what it means for a city to have a negative elevation. Give an example.

EXPERIENCE 44

• •

Why Is This Graph Misleading?

Number Sense Focus

- Reasonableness
- Relative size

Number Focus

- Activity 1: Whole numbers

Mathematical Background

• •

Graph-reading skills are assuming greater importance with the popularity of graphing calculators. Correct use of this technology requires an understanding of how to read and use scales. Graphs can be deceiving. Although a graph may report data accurately, care needs to be taken to ensure that the data and pictures in the graph are consistent.

Using the Activity

• •

1. Show the picture graph, and ask students to examine and interpret it. Students have given these interpretations:
   - "In 1930, there were 2 billion people in the world."
   - "The population in 1975 was greater than in 1930."
   - "The world population was double in 1975 what it was in 1930."
   - "World population is increasing."

2. Make a list of students' interpretations, and encourage discussion to clarify them.

3. Discuss the questions on the transparency.

Solutions

1. World population doubled from 2 billion to 4 billion people over the 45-year span from 1930 to 1975.

2. Perhaps, but it could be misleading.

3. Both the width and the height of the picture of the earth have been doubled. Thus the area of the 1975 circle is four times that of the 1930 circle. (A graph similar to the one shown in this lesson was used in a national assessment; many students had difficulty deciding what was misleading about the graph. Many failed to realize that when both dimensions are doubled, the area of the figure increases by a factor of 4. If all three dimensions—height, width, and length—were doubled, the volume would increase by a factor of 8.)

4. Possible answer: Show data in a bar graph, so the bars are a constant width and only the height is doubled.

5. It seems safe to estimate that world population will increase, but efforts to control population growth may change the doubling pattern.

Extending the Activity

- Have students conduct a survey or collect some data, report these data accurately, and design a graph that might be misinterpreted or distort the results.

- Examine newspapers and magazines for other examples of misleading graphs. Share them with your class, describing what makes them misleading and what corrections should be made.

- Ask students to research the current world population figure and growth pattern.

Why Is This Graph Misleading?

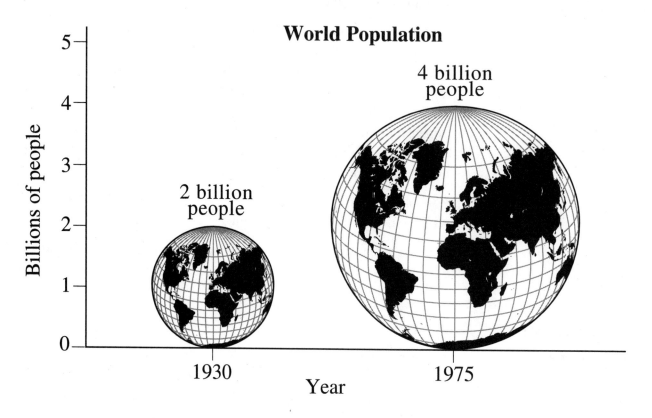

World Population

4 billion
people

2 billion
people

Billions of people

1930   1975

Year

1. What interpretations or conclusions can you make from this graph?

2. Is this graph accurately displaying the data?

3. Why is this graph misleading? Explain.

4. How would you change the graph to reflect the data more accurately?

5. What do you predict world population to be in the year 2020? How would the graph look?

Where's the Point?

Number Sense Focus

• Reasonableness

Number Focus

• Activities 1—3: Decimals

Mathematical Background

Decimal number sense requires a good understanding of place value and the relative size of numbers as related to the position of the decimal point.

Using the Activities

In these activities, students are presented with sentences containing numbers to which they may need to add a decimal point to make the sentences reasonable.

1. Reveal the first sentence of Activity 1, and invite students to decide whether a decimal point is needed to make the sentence reasonable and, if so, where it should be placed. Encourage students to give reasons for their decision.

2. Discuss each of the other sentences in turn. Students have offered explanations such as these:

   • "There are 100¢ to a dollar, and since 1475 is not quite 1500, the correct answer is not quite $15.00."

   • "Half of 5 is $2\frac{1}{2}$, so this must be 2.5."

3. Use Activities 2 and 3 in the same way.

Solutions

Activity 1

1. $5.00   2. $15.00   3. 37.4   4. 13.00   5. 2.5
6. .3   7. 1.35   8. .47   9. 100.0 10. 1.00

Activity 2

1. 4.5   2. .25   3. 1.55   4. 1.62   5. 1.5
6. 55.5 7. 55.5 8. 6.25   9. 10.95 10. 2.5

Activity 3

1. 5.5, 114.5   6. 9.9
2. 2.5, $2.45   7. 1.25 or .125
3. 9.25, 10.25, $19.50   8. $6.00 or $60.00
4. 1.0, $1.00   9. 430.5, 8.5
5. $1.80   10. 2.25

Extending the Activities

- Ask students to search the newspaper for examples of quantities involving decimals.

- Challenge students to name objects that are about each of the following lengths: 1000 m, 100 m, 10 m, 1 m, 0.1 m, 0.01 m, and 0.001 m.

Where's the Point?

Place decimal points in the numbers, if necessary, to make each sentence correct.

1. 500¢ = $500

2. 1475¢ is not quite $1500

3. 374 ÷ 10 = 374

4. 1300 ÷ 100 = 1300

5. 5 ÷ 2 = 25

6. One third is roughly 3

7. 135 centimeters = 135 meters

8. 47 centimeters = 47 meters

9. 1000 millimeters = 1000 centimeters

10. 1000 millimeters = 100 meters

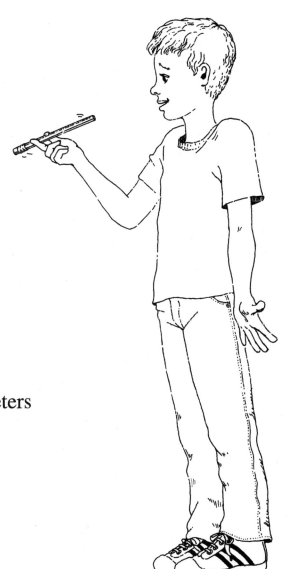

Where's the Point?

Place decimal points in the numbers, if necessary, to make each sentence correct.

1. Half of 9 is 45.

2. 25 is the same as one fourth.

3. 155 is a little more than one and a half.

4. My height is about 162 meters.

5. I bought a 15-liter bottle of cola.

6. I weigh about 555 kilograms.

7. Some eggs weigh 555 grams.

8. $2.5 \times 2.5 = 625$

9. The sprinter ran 100 meters in 1095 seconds.

10. The chicken weighed 25 kilograms.

Where's the Point?

Place decimal points in the numbers, if necessary, to make each sentence correct.

1. Hi! My name is James. I am 55 feet tall and weigh 1145 pounds.

2. We have a special sale for you: 25-pound chickens are only $245 each!

3. Turkeys between 925 and 1025 kilograms are only $1950.

4. 10-liter bottles of grapefruit juice are only $100.

5. Eggs are $180 a dozen.

6. The Olympic skater got a 99 from two of the judges.

7. Last month retail prices rose 125%

8. My sister is earning $600 per hour.

9. On our road trip, we averaged 4305 miles per day. Each day we spent 85 hours in the car.

10. Including half time, the football game lasted for 225 hours.

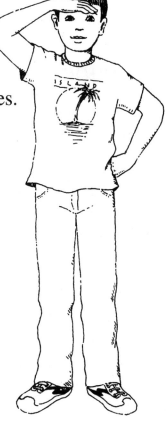

EXPERIENCE 46

• •

Why Are These Wrong?

Number Sense Focus

- Reasonableness
- Estimation

Number Focus

- Activity 1: Decimals, whole numbers

Mathematical Background

• •

When we are dealing with money, benchmarks can help us to determine reasonableness. For example, if three items cost $0.89 each, we can reason that the total cost should be less than $3. In this case, $1 serves as a benchmark for one item. Focusing on such benchmark values helps us easily establish a minimum and maximum cost.

Using the Activity

• •

In this activity, students judge the reasonableness of monetary values.

1. Show the sale sign. As a warm-up, ask students which items could be purchased with a $5 bill (a CD), a $10 bill (two CDs or one calculator), a $20 bill (a video, two calculators, one calculator and two CDs, or four CDs).

2. Ask additional questions to encourage students to think further about the information in the sign, such as: Would two CDs cost more or less than $10? Why? Would a video and a calculator cost more or less than $20? $30? Explain.

3. Have students examine the questions and decide why each bill is incorrect. Ask them to think about how the error in each bill might have resulted. Establish that reasonableness involves a thoughtful interpretation of prices and the number of items bought.

Solutions

1. CDs are less than $5 each, so the cost for two should be under $10. The bill is the price of two CDs at their regular price, $14.85.

2. A video costs $19.95, which should be the bill. A bill for $59.85 is the regular price of the video.

3. A calculator is almost $9, so two calculators is about $18, and a CD would make the cost over $20. A bill of $18.78 is the cost of two CDs and a calculator.

4. A calculator is less than $10, so three calculators should be less than $30. A bill of $59.85 is the cost of three videos.

5. CDs cost less than $5 each, so the cost for five should be under $25. The video is less than $20, so the total price should be less than $45. A bill of $104.70 is the price of five videos and a CD.

Extending the Activity

• •

- Ask groups of students to make up another problem with an unreasonable total and exchange problems with another group.

- Ask students to relate a personal experience involving an unreasonable answer and to explain why they knew it was unreasonable.

Why Are These Wrong?

Judge the reasonableness of each of these statements, and explain how you think each bill was computed.

1. Kelly bought two CDs and was charged $29.70.

2. Katasha bought a video. The clerk charged her $59.85.

3. Luis bought two calculators and a CD, and the bill was $18.78.

4. Rena bought three calculators and was charged $59.85.

5. Roberto bought five CDs and a video. The bill was $104.70.

How Many Digits in Sums?

Number Sense Focus

- Reasonableness
- Mental computation
- Relative size

Number Focus

- Activities 1—3: Whole numbers

Mathematical Background

Recognizing that the number of digits in a sum depends on the number of digits in each addend provides an early check for reasonableness of a sum.

Using the Activities

Students should have calculators for these activities.

1. Ask for examples of one-, two-, three- and four-digit numbers. Encourage students to discuss patterns and similarities. For example, the largest one-, two-, three-, and four-digit numbers (9, 99, 999, and 9999) have only 9s; the smallest two-, three-, and four-digit numbers (10, 100, 1000) have only 1s and 0s.

2. Discuss the questions in Activity 1 as a class. Encourage students to pick any two numbers (not only those shown on the transparency) with the specified number of digits and add them. You may want to make a list of the different pairs and their sums for the entire class to see. Here are some pairs of one-digit numbers and their sums:

    $5 + 6 = 11$ $2 + 7 = 9$ $3 + 8 = 11$ $9 + 9 = 18$

    $8 + 8 = 16$ $0 + 4 = 4$ $8 + 1 = 9$ $0 + 0 = 0$

This list suggests that when adding two one-digit numbers, the sum is either one or two digits. The largest sum, 18, has two digits; the smallest sum, 0, has one digit. The addition of two one-digit numbers could be represented with placeholders, such as $\bigcirc + \square =$ _____ . Any single-digit number could be placed in the $\bigcirc$ and in the $\square$ symbols, with the result always being either a one- or two-digit sum. These could be shown horizontally or vertically: $\bigcirc + \square =$ or

$$\begin{array}{r} \bigcirc \\ + \ \square \\ \hline \end{array}$$

3. In Activities 2 and 3, again ask students to choose pairs of numbers with the specified number of digits and then add the pairs. Organize the sums for the whole class to see. Ask students to describe patterns that relate the number of digits in the two addends to the number of digits in the sum. Again, symbolic notation could be used to express the operation, with any two-digit number being placed in the $\bigcirc \bigcirc$ and any two-digit number placed in the $\square \square$: $\bigcirc \bigcirc + \square \square =$ or

$$\begin{array}{r} \bigcirc \bigcirc \\ + \ \square \square \\ \hline \end{array}$$

4. Once all three activities have been completed, discuss patterns that were observed across the activities.

Solutions

This table shows one way to organize the data collected from the three activities; developing such a table with the class may be worthwhile.

| | | *Number of digits in first addend* | | | |
		1	*2*	*3*	*4*
Number	1	1 or 2	2 or 3	3 or 4	4 or 5
of digits	2	2 or 3	2 or 3	3 or 4	4 or 5
in second	3	3 or 4	3 or 4	3 or 4	4 or 5
addend	4	4 or 5	4 or 5	4 or 5	4 or 5

Extending the Activities

• •

- Ask students to make a conjecture to predict the number of digits in the sum of two five-digit whole numbers, and to describe the pattern used in the conjecture.

- Ask students to make a conjecture to predict the number of digits in the sum of any two whole numbers if they know the number of digits in each addend. What about the sum of three whole numbers?

How Many Digits in Sums?

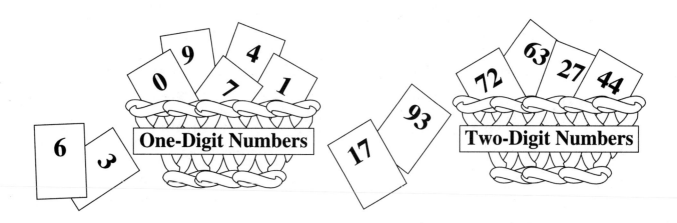

1. Choose any two one-digit numbers. How many digits are in the sum of your two numbers?

2. Keep adding pairs of one-digit numbers until you find a pattern. Describe the pattern. Say what you can about the smallest sum and the greatest sum of any two one-digit numbers.

3. Repeat the process for pairs consisting of a one-digit number and a two-digit number.

How Many Digits in Sums?

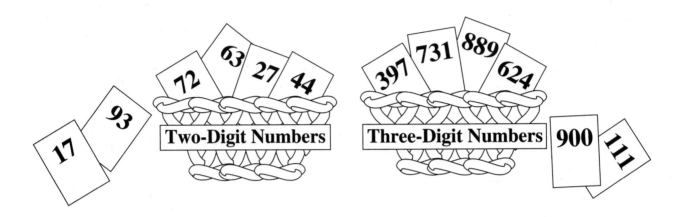

1. Choose any two two-digit numbers. How many digits are in the sum of your two numbers?

2. Repeat the process until you find a pattern. Describe the pattern. Say what you can about the smallest sum and the greatest sum of any two two-digit numbers.

3. Repeat the process for pairs consisting of a two-digit number and a three-digit number.

How Many Digits in Sums?

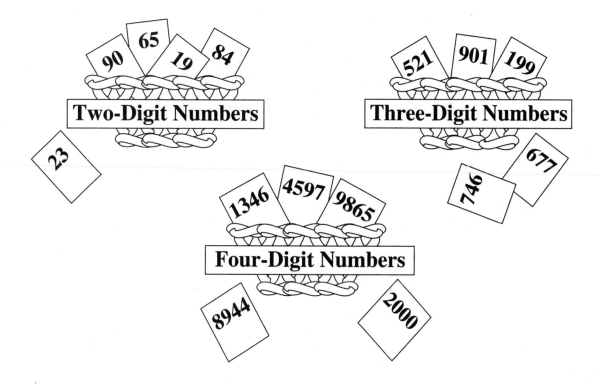

1. Choose any two four-digit numbers. How many digits are in the sum of your two numbers?

2. Repeat the process until you find a pattern. Describe the pattern. Say what you can about the smallest sum and the greatest sum of any two four-digit numbers.

3. Repeat the process for pairs consisting of a two-digit number and a four-digit number.

4. Repeat the process for pairs consisting of a three-digit number and a four-digit number.

EXPERIENCE 48

• •

How Many Digits in Products?

Number Sense Focus

- Reasonableness
- Mental computation
- Relative size

Number Focus

- Activities 1–3: Whole numbers

Mathematical Background

• •

Both the number of digits and the operation influence the size of a computational result. Relationships between the number of digits and addition were explored in Experience 48. Different relationships exist for the number of digits in the factors and their product.

Using the Activities

• •

Experience 48 should have been completed before this activity. Students will need calculators for this activity as well.

1. Discuss the questions in Activity 1 as a class. Again, symbols may be used in these activities to provide a visual frame of reference.

$$\bigcirc \times \square = \quad \text{or} \quad \begin{array}{r} \bigcirc \\ \times \ \square \\ \hline \end{array}$$

$$\bigcirc\,\bigcirc \times \square\,\square = \quad \text{or} \quad \begin{array}{r} \bigcirc\,\bigcirc \\ \times \ \square\,\square \\ \hline \end{array}$$

$$\bigcirc \times \square\,\square\,\square = \quad \text{or} \quad \begin{array}{r} \bigcirc \\ \times \ \square\,\square\,\square \\ \hline \end{array}$$

2. In Activities 2 and 3, ask students to describe patterns that relate the number of digits in two factors to the number of digits in the product.

Solutions

Many patterns may be used to describe the relationship between the number of digits in two factors and the number of digits in their product. This table shows one way to organize the data collected from the three activities; developing such a table with the class may be worthwhile.

		Number of digits in first factor			
		1	*2*	*3*	*4*
Number	1	1 or 2	2 or 3	3 or 4	4 or 5
of digits	2	2 or 3	3 or 4	4 or 5	5 or 6
in second	3	3 or 4	4 or 5	5 or 6	6 or 7
factor	4	4 or 5	5 or 6	6 or 7	7 or 8

Extending the Activities

- Ask students: What is the significance of the sign that says, "None of our factors are zero"?

- Have students make a conjecture to predict the number of digits in the product of two five-digit whole numbers, and to describe the pattern they used to make their conjecture.

- Ask students to make a conjecture to predict the number of digits in the product of any two whole numbers if they know the number of digits in each factor. What about the product of three whole numbers?

How Many Digits in Products?

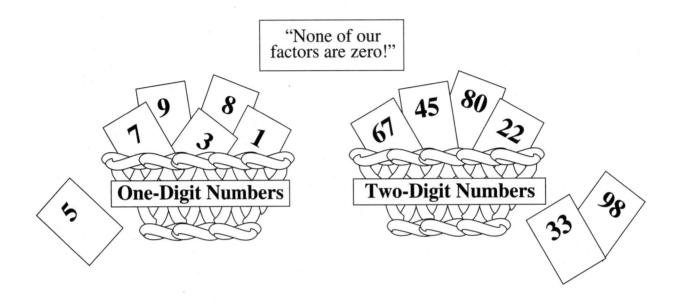

1. Choose any two one-digit numbers. How many digits are in the product of your two numbers?

2. Keep multiplying pairs of one-digit numbers until you find a pattern. Describe the pattern. Say what you can about the smallest product and the largest product of any two one-digit numbers.

3. Repeat the process for pairs consisting of a one-digit number and a two-digit number.

How Many Digits in Products?

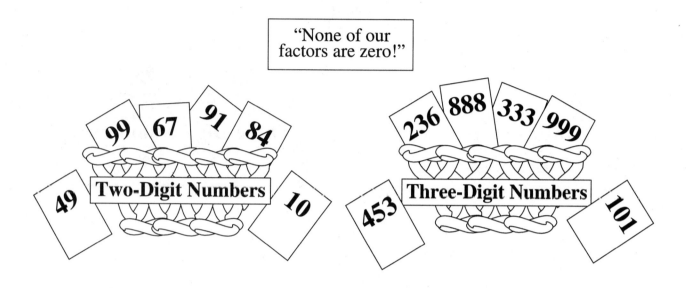

1. Choose any two two-digit numbers. How many digits are in the product of your two numbers?

2. Repeat the process until you find a pattern. Describe the pattern. Say what you can about the smallest product and the largest product of any two two-digit numbers.

3. Repeat the process for pairs consisting of a two-digit number and a three-digit number.

4. Repeat the process for pairs of three-digit numbers.

How Many Digits in Products?

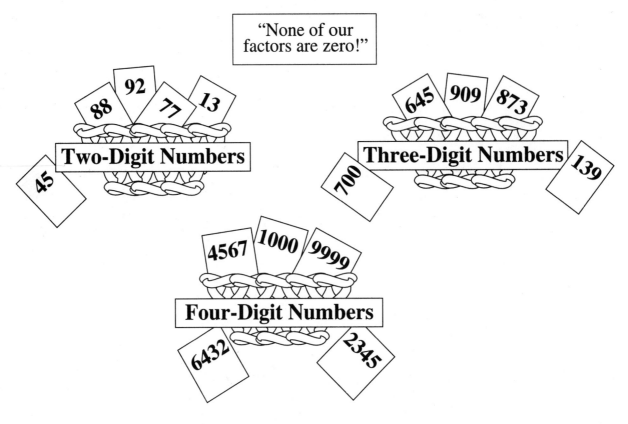

"None of our factors are zero!"

1. Choose any two four-digit numbers. How many digits are in the product of your two numbers?

2. Repeat the process until you find a pattern. Describe the pattern. Say what you can about the smallest product and the largest product of any two four-digit numbers.

3. Repeat the process for pairs consisting of a two-digit number and a four-digit number.

4. Repeat the process for pairs consisting of a three-digit number and a four-digit number.